BECAUSE I WAS
A GIRL

BECAUSE I WAS A GIRL

TRUE STORIES FOR GIRLS OF ALL AGES

EDITED BY MELISSA DE LA CRUZ

Henry Holt and Company

NEW YORK

Henry Holt and Company, *Publishers since 1866*
Henry Holt® is a registered trademark of Macmillan Publishing Group, LLC
175 Fifth Avenue, New York, NY 10010
fiercereads.com

Library of Congress Control Number: 2017934604

ISBN 978-1-250-15446-0

Our books may be purchased in bulk for promotional, educational, or business use. Please contact your local bookseller or the Macmillan Corporate and Premium Sales Department at (800) 221-7945 ext. 5442 or by e-mail at MacmillanSpecialMarkets@macmillan.com.

First edition, 2017
Book design by Rebecca Syracuse
Printed in the United States of America
10 9 8 7 6 5 4 3 2 1

FOR MY MOM AND POP, WHO MADE ME THE GIRL I AM
TODAY, AND FOR CHRISTIAN TRIMMER, KINDRED SPIRIT,
BRILLIANT EDITOR, AND GREAT FRIEND

—MELISSA DE LA CRUZ

CONTENTS

THE 1920s-1930s 8

DOLORES HUERTA 10

BONNIE BARTLETT 16

THE 1940s 22

GLORIA MOLINA 24

SUSAN MORRISON 30

WILLIABEL JONES DAVIS 34

THE 1950s 40

TRISH McEVOY 42

MARGARET SEMRUD-CLIKEMAN 46

CHERI STEINKELLNER 52

BRENDA BOWEN 58

FRANCESCA ZAMBELLO 64

BABETTE DAVIS 70

HOLLY KNIGHT 74

THE 1960s 80

MARGARET STOHL 82

ANNA PONDER 88

JILL LORIE 94

KATRINA ADAMS 100

LIBBA BRAY 106

THE 1970s   114

MELISSA DE LA CRUZ   116

ABBY FALIK   122

REBECCA SOFFER   128

TINA HAY   136

ANJANETTE JOHNSTON   142

ZAREEN JAFFERY   148

THE 1980s   154

ELIZABETH ACEVEDO   156

JENA FRIEDMAN   162

EMILY CALANDRELLI   166

JANE HAWLEY   172

JODY HOUSER   178

LORETTA MIRANDA   182

LENORE ZION   188

KATIE BUTTON   194

THE 1990s   200

VICTORIA AVEYARD   202

JOAN HANAWI   208

NOOR TAGOURI   214

TILLIE WALDEN   218

THE 2000s   226

QUVENZHANÉ WALLIS   228

ZOEY LUNA   232

MATTIE JOHNSTON   238

THE 2010s   242

CONTRIBUTORS   246

SUPPORT GIRLS AND WOMEN AROUND THE WORLD   254

SPECIAL THANKS   256

THE 1920s-1930s

- THE UNITED STATES RATIFIES THE NINETEENTH AMENDMENT, GRANTING WOMEN THE RIGHT TO VOTE AFTER AN APPROXIMATE SEVENTY-YEAR BATTLE FOR VOTING RIGHTS BY SUFFRAGISTS.

- IN 1925, THE FIRST WOMAN'S WORLD'S FAIR, A FAIR RUN ENTIRELY BY WOMEN, WAS HELD IN CHICAGO AND DISPLAYED THE PROGRESS OF IDEAS, WORK, AND INVENTIONS OF TWENTIETH-CENTURY WOMEN.

- THOUGH THE GREAT DEPRESSION LEAVES 12 MILLION PEOPLE OUT OF WORK, WOMEN MAKE UP 24 PERCENT OF THE LABOR FORCE, MOSTLY AS NURSES, TELEPHONE OPERATORS, AND TEACHERS.

- WOMEN ENTER THE WORKFORCE AT A RATE TWICE THAT OF MEN BECAUSE EMPLOYERS CAN HIRE THEM AT REDUCED WAGES.

- DOROTHY THOMPSON, AN AMERICAN JOURNALIST AND RADIO BROADCASTER, IS THE FIRST JOURNALIST TO BE EXPELLED FROM NAZI GERMANY FOR CRITICIZING HITLER AS "THE VERY PROTOTYPE OF THE LITTLE MAN."

- LIZZIE MAGIE PHILLIPS INVENTS A BOARD GAME, THE LANDLORD'S GAME, TO CRITIQUE BIG BUSINESS. THE GAME WILL BE RELEASED UNDER A DIFFERENT NAME: MONOPOLY.

- PEARL S. BUCK, THE FIRST AMERICAN WOMAN TO WIN THE NOBEL PRIZE IN LITERATURE, PUBLISHES HER NOVEL *THE GOOD EARTH*, A DRAMATIZATION OF FAMILY LIFE IN A CHINESE VILLAGE, AND ADVOCATES FOR THE RIGHTS OF WOMEN AND MINORITY GROUPS.

- ANNA MAY WONG, THE FIRST CHINESE-AMERICAN MOVIE STAR, PLAYS OPPOSITE MARLENE DIETRICH IN JOSEF VON STERNBERG'S OSCAR-WINNING *SHANGHAI EXPRESS*.

DOLORES HUERTA

When I was young, my mother, a feminist, treated my brothers and me equally: We all had to do the dishes, cook, and make the beds.

I was lucky to have been raised by my mother, Alicia St. John Chavez, a divorced single parent who had strong social values. Machismo was not present in my family. My mom was a businesswoman who set high expectations for all of us. She wasn't overprotective, though. As long as we did our chores, we could have free recreational time. I had a great childhood. Mom was always pushing me to achieve, and I felt she favored me over my brothers. My mom said that girls needed more support.

My father was a volunteer union organizer. Everyplace that he worked, he organized a union. I am my father's daughter, although I was not raised by him.

I was shy, but joining the Girl Scouts helped me overcome that. I was a Girl Scout from the ages of eight to eighteen. I had a wonderful Girl Scout leader, Kathryn Kemp—she encouraged and supported me. I learned many important life lessons and skills with the Girl Scouts that I would carry with me throughout my life.

As a young woman, I was introduced to organizing at a house meeting by Mr. Fred Ross Sr. We formed a group called the Community Service Organization (CSO). He showed us how ordinary working people could organize and make improvements in their community.

That is where I learned how to organize people and communities. That's when I realized that organizing is what I wanted to do. I later left the CSO to found the United Farm Workers union with Cesar Chavez, a grassroots movement focused on improving the lives of workers who place food on America's tables.

There were challenges, though. I had been raised in a middle-class household, and I was now working and organizing farm workers. It was a culture shift for me.

I was always working, and my mother-in-law wanted to know why I couldn't stay home with the kids. My husband's family would criticize me, ask why I was out there organizing, dragging the kids to meetings and rallies. But I was lucky. I had people to help take care of my children—my mom helped and I always had babysitters. My paycheck went directly to my babysitters. In the farm workers union, we set up a child-care center for union members who worked outside the home.

I tell young women to follow their passions, to not let anyone get in their way, to stand up for themselves always, and to reach out and stand up for others. Time is the most precious resource we have—use it to make the world a better place, help the people who need help.

In 2002, I founded my own organization, the Dolores Huerta Foundation, and went back to community organizing. We work on health care; education; infrastructure; getting people to run for office, water district boards, and school district boards; immigrant and human rights; and organizing people in their communities. When President Obama awarded me with the Presidential Medal

I TELL YOUNG WOMEN TO FOLLOW THEIR **PASSIONS,** TO NOT LET ANYONE GET **IN THEIR WAY,** TO STAND UP FOR THEMSELVES ALWAYS, AND TO REACH OUT **AND STAND UP FOR OTHERS.**

WHEN PRESIDENT OBAMA AWARDED ME WITH THE PRESIDENTIAL MEDAL OF FREEDOM IN 2012, I WAS PROUD TO BE RECOGNIZED AS A COMMUNITY ORGANIZER BECAUSE HE WAS ONE, TOO.

of Freedom in 2012, I was proud to be recognized as a community organizer because he was one, too.

I think we'll come out okay from the current presidential administration. I lived through the 1960s and 1970s, when environmental issues, the women's movement, and the Chicano movement were just starting. Now all these organizations have strong foundations and leadership, which we didn't have when Nixon was president.

We're going to come out on top—not just survive but come out stronger as a community, as a people, as a country. ¡Sí Se Puede!

BONNIE BARTLETT

grew up in Moline, Illinois, which is right on the border of Iowa. At
the time, it was a town of only 35,000 people and sat in the middle
of mostly farmland. The biggest employer was the John Deere tractor
company. In such a place, and at such a time (the 1930s), it was natural
that there would be old-fashioned values dictating the ways in which men
and women treated each other. Specifically, when it came to women—or
girls—there was an understanding that men—or boys—were superior. My
own family was no exception; my older brother, Bob, was the recipient
of most of the attention that my parents could muster. They didn't have
much money, but whatever they had went toward my brother's future. At
one point, in fact, money they had put aside for my education was given
to my brother so he could attend military school.

All of this made me want to become a boy. My mother would put me
in beautiful lace-trimmed dresses, and I would come back inside from
playing, my clothes completely torn and covered in dirt. I would get into
fights with the 11th Avenue C Boys, a gang of tough street kids, and could

not only take a punch but also deliver one. My father purchased a pair of boxing gloves for my brother—I put them on one day and knocked my brother out. I was determined to be no little princess waiting for her prince to come and wake her with a kiss.

My plan to be another "son" to my mother and father completely fell apart when I was ten years old and experienced a very early puberty. I was ashamed of the bleeding and burned all of my underwear. It was clear that I was going to be female the rest of my life, but that didn't stop me from continuing my drive for independence. My father wanted me to become a teacher, but I had discovered something that would become my life's passion: acting. (Ironically, my father was a professional actor when he was younger, and he's the one who gave me my love for the theater.) When my parents finally decided to pay for my education, my mother offered to send me to St. Catherine's, an all-girls school. I would have none of that; if I was going to be a great actress, playing great women's roles, I was *not* going to play male roles as might be required at St. Catherine's.

When I was about to enter high school, my father took me down into the basement and told me that he couldn't afford to send me to college. He said I would have to earn a scholarship. And so I worked diligently at my grades . . . and graduated as valedictorian. After graduation, I wanted to go to New York City to study at the prestigious Neighborhood Playhouse, but my father wouldn't allow me to go there by myself at the age of eighteen. And so I enrolled (with a scholarship) at Northwestern University.

I finally made it to New York four years later, filled with confidence. I picked up the want ads and found jobs, and from the start I made it clear to my bosses that I would not put up with any kind of misogyny or harassment. For that reason, some of the jobs didn't last long. But I didn't care, because I had a sense of my own worth and knew there would be something else. In 1955, I landed my first big role and was earning $1,000 per week (this was a huge amount of money then), but I still couldn't change the attitudes of the men in my Moline

I WAS DETERMINED TO BE NO LITTLE **PRINCESS** WAITING FOR HER PRINCE TO COME AND **WAKE HER** WITH A KISS.

PICKED UP THE WANT ADS AND FOUND JOBS, AND FROM THE START I MADE IT CLEAR TO MY BOSSES THAT I WOULD NOT PUT UP WITH **ANY KIND** OF MISOGYNY OR **HARASSMENT.** FOR THAT REASON, SOME OF **THE JOBS DIDN'T LAST LONG.**

family. My brother shocked me by saying, "You aren't worth more than $75 per week, just like any other secretary." And I could never win my father's approval. In spite of my success, he still thought I should be working as a teacher until I could produce babies. (I'm sure there was also a lot of jealousy over the fact that he was no longer acting.)

I continued to work very hard at my craft and eventually became a TV star. My struggles as a girl came in very handy—even when I found myself at the top of my profession, I still had to stand up for myself. I remember vividly a producer who made promises that he broke, and he only changed his mind because I argued with him—loudly and passionately the way a man would. The argument wasn't about money—I never felt secure enough to ask for more money—but it has to be noted that women in show business have never been paid as much as men. The greatest actress in our profession, Meryl Streep, is still paid less than male stars.

As I write this, I'm in my eighties, and I continue to work in film and on television shows. I've been acting for sixty years, but looking back, the happiest times of my life were as a mother. When you're a mother, no one can really tell you what to do—you find your own way. I didn't like being forced to be "a girl," but I certainly enjoyed becoming a woman.

THE 1940s

- HEDY LAMARR, AN AUSTRIAN IMMIGRANT AND FAMOUS FILM ACTRESS, INVENTS A JAM-PROOF RADIO-GUIDANCE SYSTEM FOR TORPEDOES THAT IS NOW USED IN MODERN WI-FI AND CELL PHONE TECHNOLOGY.

- THE UNITED NATIONS ESTABLISHES THE COMMISSION ON THE STATUS OF WOMEN TO PROTECT WOMEN'S POLITICAL, ECONOMIC, CIVIL, SOCIAL, AND EDUCATIONAL RIGHTS.

- CHICAGO CUBS OWNER PHILIP WRIGLEY FOUNDS THE ALL-AMERICAN GIRLS PROFESSIONAL BASEBALL LEAGUE TO FILL BALLPARKS EMPTIED BY BASEBALL PLAYERS GOING TO WAR.

- AFRICAN-AMERICAN PERFORMER JOSEPHINE BAKER WORKS AS A SPY IN FRANCE, HELPING THE RESISTANCE BY SMUGGLING MESSAGES TO FRENCH SOLDIERS WITH INVISIBLE INK ON HER SHEET MUSIC.

- DURING WORLD WAR II, MORE THAN 350,000 WOMEN CONTRIBUTE TO THE WAR EFFORT AS MILITARY PERSONNEL.

- ROSIE THE RIVETER BECOMES AN ICON REPRESENTING THE MORE THAN SIX MILLION WOMEN WHO ENTER THE WORKFORCE, MANY IN INDUSTRIAL JOBS, BECAUSE OF THE WAR.

- GERTY CORI, AFTER BEING WARNED SHE MIGHT HARM HER HUSBAND'S SCIENTIFIC CAREER, WINS THE NOBEL PRIZE IN PHYSIOLOGY OR MEDICINE, SHARING THE AWARD WITH HER HUSBAND FOR THEIR COLLABORATION ON THE CATALYTIC CONVERSION OF GLYCOGEN. SHE IS PAID ONE-TENTH OF WHAT HER HUSBAND RECEIVES IN SALARY.

POLITICIAN
Photo credit: Martin Zamora

GLORIA MOLINA

"We already decided who is running for the congressional seats and will let you know when a woman will run." As a Chicana, Latina, Hispanic woman, I was shocked to hear that response from the controlling political group of men. This was 1981, a time when elective office for Latinas was just a dream. A large increase in the Latino population had created two congressional seats in the Eastside of Los Angeles. In our naïveté, we thought, here is the perfect opportunity to get the first Hispanic woman in the United States Congress. It only made sense to us to select one woman and one man for those two open seats. But no, the Latino men who held positions of power in Los Angeles informed us that two men would fill the seats. As a Chicana who had actively supported and organized volunteers to get Latino men elected in our community, I was devastated by the pronouncement.

The Latino community had made great strides against gerrymandering, racism, intimidation, and lack of political resources. We were finally getting opportunities to compete in various political seats. It was not automatic—we marched, we organized, and we empowered ourselves to overcome the hurdles of getting Latinos elected to political office. Latinas in our communities were shoulder to shoulder with the men in all those efforts. So their pronouncement—*not yet, we will let you know when*—was disheartening.

Totally unprepared for the callous and abrupt response, our small cadre of Latinas regrouped. While this was a setback, it put us on a path of strategic action. Leading up to this time, Chicana feminists were actively involved in two significant movements—the Chicano movement, which was a call to action to the overconcentration of Latinos on the front lines in Vietnam and the inequality of opportunity for Latinos, and the feminist movement, which was fighting for women's rights but was basically a white women's movement that did not respect or understand racism in minority communities.

As Latinas, we aspired for opportunity in the Latino community, and we were exploring, discussing, and raising awareness that the traditional role for women in our community was totally unacceptable. We, too, wanted to provide leadership and harness political and economic power. While supportive of these two movements, we started our own unique organization, Comisión Femenil Mexicana. Our goal was to empower ourselves and advocate for the Latina and her family. We also founded the Chicana Service Action Center, an employment training center, and Centro de Niños, a bilingual, bicultural child-care center. Latinas needed better employment opportunities and security of their children's well-being while they studied and worked.

We decided to push back. We informed the men that we *would* have a female candidate for the legislative seat and quickly went into action. While it had been my goal to manage the campaign, I ended up the candidate. We recognized the challenges of running against the men in our community, which included a lack of resources and endorsements. But facing those challenges, we strategized for each of them. It was not the first time that we Latinas recognized we would have to work twice as hard to be equal.

WE NEEDED TO DEMONSTRATE TO THE MEN IN OUR COMMUNITY THAT THEY COULD NOT TAKE US FOR GRANTED AND THAT WE WERE A FORCE TO BE RECKONED WITH.

THE PRESSURE WAS NEARLY UNBEARABLE. BUT DISPROVING THAT WE HAD TO WAIT OUR TURN WAS A POWERFUL MOTIVATOR. WE FOUND OUR COURAGE AND DETERMINATION. WE DEALT WITH THE SETBACKS AND PURSUED OUR GOAL WITH PASSION AND FORTITUDE.

We built a campaign on the strengths of women. We reached out to the many female political networks and female elected officials that many of us had also supported throughout the years. We called everyone we knew and asked for money, we called on every volunteer we had ever recruited, and we hired a female political consultant. While we did not have the money our opponent had, we had volunteers and passion. We walked door-to-door every day of the campaign, we raised money, we sent handwritten notes and mailers. We assessed and reassessed each and every day. We struggled, we had setbacks and disappointments, but we knew we had to make every effort to win or at least run a competitive effort. We needed to demonstrate to the men in our community that they could not take us for granted and that we were a force to be reckoned with. We fought discrimination from men and women in our community as they, too, had bought into the stereotype of Latinas' role in positions of power. We heard comments like "I would never vote for a woman," "A woman cannot handle pressure," and "I do not trust a woman representing me in the political arena." Even Latinas in our community doubted our ability to win. The stakes were high, and we deeply understood that losing the campaign would be a tremendous setback for all women. The pressure was nearly unbearable. But disproving that we had to wait our turn was a powerful motivator. We found our courage and determination. We dealt with the setbacks and pursued our goal with passion and fortitude.

In 1982, I was elected as the first Latina to the California legislature. I have proudly served my community for more than 30 years as a member of the legislature, the Los Angeles City Council, and the Los Angeles County Board of Supervisors. We kicked the door open for many well-qualified Latinas to serve in the legislature, Congress, or local office. I have been followed by many unbelievably qualified Latinas to serve in significant political positions. No longer would the political bullies of our community say to any woman, "Because you are a girl, you must wait until we decide when you can take a position of power."

BISHOP

SUSAN MORRISON

In the history of the worldwide United Methodist Church, there had been only three women elected to the episcopacy. One woman had been elected in 1980, the other two in 1984. All three elections came after years of strategizing by women, including myself, trying to get a woman to be even considered as a possible bishop.

At the 1988 quadrennial Jurisdictional Conference, where new bishops are elected to replace retirees, the Northeastern Jurisdiction in the United States was to elect one bishop. Never had a woman been elected in that jurisdiction. That year, many male candidates and one woman were in the running. Brochures and campaign buttons were being distributed, and candidates were interviewed as the hopefuls seeking election vied for the combined lay and clergy delegate votes.

I was not planning to attend that regional gathering. Just two months earlier at a worldwide denominational conference, I had been elected to the

Judicial Council, the denomination's "Supreme Court." I was the first clergy-woman ever to hold that position. However, a phone call motivated me to attend since I was the lone regional member on the Judicial Council. So, at the last minute, I packed some casual clothes in a bag and off I went.

The voting began. To win the election, a candidate needed more than 60 percent of the delegates' votes. Each delegate could vote for one of the listed can-didates, but there was a possibility of write-in votes. After the first two ballots, it was clear the clergywoman candidate we had managed to get on the ballot was receiving little support. On the third ballot report, I heard a familiar name: *Susan Morrison, one vote. My* name! Amused, I wondered which friend had written it. On the next ballot, I received two votes. On the next ballot, there were seventeen votes!

And then the drama began.

Question from the Chair: *Now that Susan Morrison has received more than ten votes, will a biographical sheet be distributed?*

Answer: *Not at this time.*

On this third day of the Jurisdictional Conference, I was an unexpected, un-prepared candidate for the episcopacy. Frankly, I was stunned. As the morning session drew to a close, four women converged on me, accompanied me to the snack bar, and began to strategize what to do. First things first, they said. The vitae sheet, the requested biographical information, needed to be prepared.

Together we thought of what should be included. Education? Church ser-vice? One of the women wrote the information down in her calligraphic script on a plain sheet of paper. Another took the final product off to be copied and distributed.

Who were those women who led me through the "what to do next" when the numbness, the precursor of the emotional shock that would come, was be-ginning to set in? There was Lynne, who had been "the woman candidate" in our jurisdiction in 1984. There was Diedra, who was "the woman candidate" in the Northeastern Jurisdiction this very year. And there were Molly and Linda, two women who had been working on Diedra's campaign. All were committed to helping a woman be elected; two of them had aspirations themselves and had anticipated what it would mean to be chosen. They had long considered the historic consecration process, had understood the enormous responsibility of administering the hundreds of churches, clergy, and conferences that is part of the position, and knew that this election was for life. Life! Each now sat with me, helping me respond.

By evening, the voting was over. I had won—a woman had been elected. The barrier of exclusion was broken. Not anticipating this in any way, I had not packed properly. The consecration service was immediately before me. My beach sandals would just have to do, but I really needed to borrow a robe and stole. Off I went to once again call on others for help. From those moments on, my life and my call to ministry were changed forever.

Out of the flashes of memory of those most unusual hours, the image of the five of us around the table in the college snack bar comes to me. A model of sisterhood . . . a symbol of female community . . . of dreams tempered with reality . . . unselfish goals . . . gifts shared . . . bonds of respect. Truly it is a vision of what I continue to hope the larger faith community can be.

WILLIABEL JONES DAVIS

I t was the 1969–1970 academic year. I was twenty-one and a senior at Virginia State College, a historically black college in Petersburg, Virginia. I was an English major with a minor in business. I wanted to be a high school teacher (or so I thought). With stacks of books to read and research papers due in every class, I didn't have much spare time.

When I did find a little time, I looked and applied for teaching positions (in Virginia and New Jersey). I found that the salaries for English teachers were not very promising; so when the army lieutenant recruiter visited our campus, I went to hear what she had to say. Only about nine or ten of us coeds showed up to see this female army recruiter.

She was impressive: medium height, slender stature, impeccably dressed, in what I would later learn was a class-B uniform. She was well-groomed; every blond hair was in place. Her makeup was perfectly applied, just a bit understated, yet highlighting her blue eyes. Her shoes had been spit-shined. She talked about joining the Women's Army Corps in particular and the army as a career in general.

The first thing that attracted me to this whole new career idea was that we would be officers, receiving a direct commission and taking the oath of office as a second lieutenant. Second, clothes would be tailored to fit perfectly. Third, and most important, the starting "base salary" was much higher than a first-year teacher's salary. In addition, there would be a housing allowance and a subsistence allowance added to the base salary. This made the monthly income considerably higher than an English teacher's salary. Plus, men and women with the same rank and time in grade received the same pay. The military obligation of active duty was only two years. After that, I could use GI Bill money to earn a master's degree and teach college students rather than high school. The decision was a no-brainer (or so I thought).

I left that meeting feeling exhilarated! I had made a decision. It would be a military career for the foreseeable future, or at least the next two years. After that, who knew? I was on cloud nine. I could hardly wait to tell my roommate, who was also a very close friend. (We would later be in each other's bridal parties.)

When I told her, she said, "Are you kidding? Do you know what kind of women are in the military?" She paused. "Dykes and hookers."

I was stunned into silence. When I found my voice, I replied, "Actually, I don't know what kind of women are in the military, since I've never been in. Anyway, the one I just finished talking to didn't seem to fit either category."

We did not speak of it again. But her words stuck with me.

I was still committed to joining, but then I faced another setback. The next emotional roadblock (a full-frontal attack) was even more disturbing. It came from one of my two older sisters, both of whom I adored. I really valued their opinions. So when my sister said similarly harsh things about women in the military that echoed my roommate's opinion, I was truly crushed.

I HAD HEARD HER SPEAK OF OUR UNCLES AND MALE COUSINS IN UNIFORM WITH SUCH PRIDE, YET SHE COULDN'T IMAGINE THAT A WOMAN—HER SISTER, EVEN—COULD GARNER THE SAME RECOGNITION.

I asked her, "Do you even know any female officers?" I knew she didn't, and she said as much. But she was worried about my "reputation," worried that I would be talked about by people who, in my opinion, didn't know what they were talking about. But she was so sure they did.

I was devastated. I had heard her speak of our uncles and male cousins in uniform with such pride, yet she couldn't imagine that a woman—her sister, even—could garner the same recognition. I knew any further conversation with her would be futile.

I headed for the one person whose point of view mattered most to me: my father, Wilbur Jones. My mother had always deferred important decisions in her girls' lives to him. She trusted his judgment completely. Her mantra was "If it's okay with your father, it's okay with me."

My father had always been my role model. He worked hard—we could count on him. He was a man of his word and a good listener. He was honest with everyone and loyal to family and friends. He was kindhearted and charitable. He had a great sense of humor. He played the guitar for fun and to entertain the family. And he had always supported his children's endeavors. Besides, unlike my roommate and sister, he had actually been in the military. After the bombing of Pearl Harbor, he had served in the navy for a couple of years during World War II.

So I told him what I was planning. I said, "Daddy, I want to talk to you. After college, I want to go into the army."

He simply said, "Yeah?"

I took that as a signal to continue. "After I graduate, and the FBI thoroughly investigates me, I will get a direct commission as a second lieutenant. My obligation will be two years of active duty. What do you think?"

In his persistent manner, my father questioned me like a seasoned prosecutor questioning a guilty but clever defendant on the witness stand, turning the matter every which way but loose. When he was satisfied that I knew what I was doing, he said, "Well, if you think that is really what you want to do, and you think you can handle it, it's okay with me."

That was all I needed to hear. I joined what turned out to be a microcosm of America. The women in the military were no different from the civilian women they grew up with. They were living proof of one of the answers I had given my father: "Daddy, I believe you take the morals you're raised with wherever you go."

Years later, when he introduced me to a friend he had not seen in many years, he said, "This is my daughter, Williabel. She is the youngest of the three, all girls. She is a college professor."

His voice changed ever so slightly with a bit more pride. "She is also a retired army lieutenant colonel."

THE 1950s

- MILLIONS OF WOMEN LOSE THEIR JOBS BECAUSE OF THE SHRINKING OF THE DEFENSE INDUSTRY AND THE RETURN OF MALE VETERANS AT THE END OF WORLD WAR II.

- WOMEN MAKE UP 30 PERCENT OF ENROLLED COLLEGE STUDENTS, A DROP FROM 47 PERCENT IN 1920, SHOWING CHANGING EXPECTATIONS OF WOMEN AS HOUSEWIVES AND MOTHERS.

- ROSA PARKS BECOMES KNOWN AS "THE MOTHER OF THE CIVIL RIGHTS MOVEMENT" AFTER SHE REFUSES TO SURRENDER HER SEAT ON A MONTGOMERY, ALABAMA, BUS.

- THE DAUGHTERS OF BILITIS, THE FIRST LESBIAN-RIGHTS ORGANIZATION IN THE UNITED STATES, IS FOUNDED IN 1957.

- *DECOY: POLICE WOMAN* AIRS IN 1957, BECOMING THE FIRST TELEVISION SHOW TO FEATURE A FEMALE POLICE OFFICER.

- AFTER THE BOSTON MARATHON BARS HER FROM ENTERING, ARLENE PIEPER ASCENDS AND DESCENDS PIKES PEAK IN THE PIKES PEAK MARATHON IN 1959, BECOMING THE FIRST WOMAN TO OFFICIALLY FINISH A MARATHON IN THE UNITED STATES.

INNOVATOR, ENTREPRENEUR,
AUTHOR, AND FOUNDER OF
TRISH McEVOY BEAUTY
Photo credit: Olivia Graham

TRISH McEVOY

O ne of my first toys was a tube of lipstick.

As a child, I lived with my grandmother who owned a perfumery in Berlin. Filled with beautiful bottles, colors, and scents, it was my Disneyland. I spent my days with grown-up women and watched how much fun they had with makeup, how *happy* it made them feel. It was an endless beauty party that I never wanted to leave.

I feel so blessed to have known what I wanted from a young age.

My first building block was at a company started by a woman but led by men. The men called the shots, but the women got the job done. *My* dream was to start a cosmetics company and *lead it with women.*

How did I do it? Part luck, part grit, and a whole lot of passionate planning. I was blessed again at the beginning of my career to meet the love of my life, a renowned New York City dermatologist, Dr. Ronald Sherman. He was my biggest fan and supported every idea I ever had. I know how lucky I was.

The first big idea came when I was working as a makeup artist and

HOW DID I DO IT? PART LUCK, PART GRIT, AND A WHOLE LOT OF PASSIONATE PLANNING.

realized that easy makeup-application tools didn't exist. So I made my own, cutting art-store paintbrushes into shapes that made it easy to get great results. I took the prototypes to a manufacturer and, one step at a time, had them crafted by the best of the best. After a joyful, painstaking process of getting everything right, I incorporated Trish McEvoy Beauty, placed a stamp-size ad in *Vogue*, and watched the orders flood in. The success of this experience gave me confidence in my vision: Maybe I am seeing something no one else has seen. Never doubt *your* ability to *Be a First*.

My husband's and my next idea was to join forces! We opened the first medi-spa to offer dermatology and makeup services under one roof. Then retailers began asking to sell my makeup. After turning down many offers, I assembled my dream team and entered my first store, Henri Bendel, on Fifth Avenue in New York City. The first year, we beat our sales goal by *five times over*! This success taught me the value of waiting to strike until the iron is *really hot*. Of trusting my gut and always being willing to walk away. Of the all-importance of a great team. *Because you can't do anything alone.*

Apart from my husband, a handful of wonderful men on my corporate team, and brilliant artists on my sales force, most of my key players over the years have been women. Women who live and breathe the thrill of makeup, from the fun of playing with color to the emotional power of conquering a flaw and turning self-criticism into confidence. Women who know that if you love what you do, you never really work a day in your life. Who support one another. Who are passionate about the power of beauty, push themselves to be the best, and care about passing the torch to others—teaching women the daily high of being their own beauty experts.

I had a dream to live a life of makeup and sisterhood. I stuck to my dream, and to this day, I have never stopped working to keep it alive. Makeup gave me not only a career but also a husband, my best friends, and my chosen family—my team.

If you have a dream, don't waste a second before chasing it. *You* are the one and only architect of your life, and the sooner you start planning and building, the sooner you will enjoy a life you love.

DIVISION DIRECTOR, CLINICAL
BEHAVIORAL NEUROSCIENCE,
UNIVERSITY OF MINNESOTA

MARGARET SEMRUD-CLIKEMAN

When I was sixteen years old, my band director placed the high school and junior high school concert bands in my hands. He was traveling to a conference, and rather than cancel class, he chose me to conduct after a few quick lessons. I was so excited about this opportunity. Upon the arrival of a faculty supervisor, I led the bands in playing a piece we had rehearsed. An overwhelming feeling came over me as the students responded to my direction. The music swelled and ebbed as I asked the different sections to play louder and then softer. It swirled around me, and I felt it become a part of me. It was an amazing, powerful feeling, unlike any I had ever felt. In that moment, I decided I would grow up to be a conductor of an orchestra—preferably high school or college—or dare I hope, a professional orchestra.

I went to college with a great deal of enthusiasm to pursue a music degree. Right away, I was told I would make a fine teacher of music at an elementary school. That is a fine profession but not the one I wanted. I continued to dream that one day I would conduct an orchestra that would make beautiful music.

After two years of foundational courses, I was ready to take my first course in professional conducting. It was a rigorous class that entailed conducting a choir made up of fellow students—very demanding as well as anxiety-producing. It was difficult to learn the musical score while simultaneously knowing when to have the sopranos sing louder and the tenors more quietly. Not only did I have to master the basic music, I had to think about how to interpret the music. Plus, it was choral music—I was more accustomed to instrumental music. On top of all that, the professor was very intimidating. It was hard to sleep the night before that class. Each time I approached the podium to conduct, my heart was in my throat.

Despite all this, I enjoyed the class and looked forward to it. I was very motivated to learn as much as I could. It helped that most of the other students felt the same way I did.

After my third turn at conducting, the professor asked me what I wanted to do after graduation. I told him I wanted to conduct a high school or college band or orchestra. He offered a patronizing smile, told me I had talent . . . and that I would make an excellent music teacher at an elementary school! I just smiled at him—I was very intimidated—and left the classroom. All night I struggled with my feelings and thought about what he had said, and what others in the music department had echoed. But at that point I had not found my voice to say authoritatively that I aspired for something else.

I had no one to talk to about my dreams, no one who would really understand what I was trying to achieve. My parents had not attended college; I was the first in my family to do so. Still, I called my mother, and she listened carefully to what I was saying and told me to go talk to the professor again. We practiced what I would say, and I finally got up the courage to make an appointment.

The big day arrived, and I approached the appointment with great trepidation. The professor listened to me carefully, and he was quite respectful. When I was done, he very kindly explained that it wasn't feminine to stand in front of an orchestra and conduct—that it would not look good and that it really was a profession for men. I felt my dreams slipping away. I tried to talk about why I wanted to be a conductor, but he told me it just wasn't an acceptable position for a woman. He again told me I would be an excellent music teacher at an elementary school!

It was all I could do not to cry as he continued to tell me how noble a profession this would be for me. I felt anger, I felt extreme sadness, and I felt hopelessness. I managed to leave with a smile and tears in my eyes and went to my dorm room to be by myself and cry.

I spent the next two weeks trying to figure out what to do. This was before the Internet, so I could not search to see how many women conducted college orchestras or bands. There was no way for me to find the very few women who held these jobs to get their advice. I decided to look at other professions and see what they might offer me.

I approached the psychology department and was fortunate to talk with the sole female professor in that group. I looked at the curriculum and decided that I could become a psychologist—there were women who were psychologists. True, at that time, not as many women as men, but at least there was an openness to my pursuing my studies. While this was a very tumultuous time in my life, it was the best decision I could have made. I finished my bachelor's degree in one and a half years (compared with the usual three) with a major in psychology and subsequently completed my master's degree in school psychology. I practiced as a school psychologist for fourteen years before pursuing my doctorate in clinical neuropsychology.

I am now a division director in Clinical Behavioral Neuroscience at the University of Minnesota and surrounded by other accomplished women.

WHEN I WAS DONE, HE VERY KINDLY EXPLAINED THAT IT WASN'T FEMININE TO STAND IN FRONT OF AN ORCHESTRA AND CONDUCT.

The only disappointment I have in my career is that all my mentors were men—no women were in supervisory roles during my education. I now aim to provide such mentorship to young women who are pursuing their advanced studies. It is a struggle as I watch my younger faculty trying to balance family life and a demanding career. But I take comfort in the fact that I can help them navigate the ways of the working world. In some ways, that narrow-minded professor did me a favor by allowing me to channel my abilities in another way.

I am sad that still extremely few women conduct college bands or orchestras and even fewer conduct professional orchestras. It took thirty-seven years from the time of my experience before a woman was selected to conduct a major orchestra. That was in 2007. As of this writing, there are only eleven women conducting professional orchestras in the world, and only five are listed among the top conductors. We still have a long way to go.

CHERI STEINKELLNER

One Saturday afternoon in the late 1960s, Papa Al took all the boys to a Dodgers game, and Nana Betty took us girls to the Valley Music Theatre to see our very first stage musical, *Peter Pan*. Now, this was back before terms like *gender bias* and *heteronormative* were invented. This was back when theater was for girls and ball games were for boys.

My cousin Cathy and I were all dressed up, in scratchy petticoats and shiny shoes. The lights go down, the orchestra tunes up, and without warning, I can't breathe. Nana Betty thinks I'm having an asthma attack. She scrambles through her Nana-bag for the inhaler. But actually it's my brother (at the ball game) who has asthma. I just can't breathe because it's my first time in a theater, and I don't know it yet, but I'm about to sneak a peek at the rest of my life.

Because I am a girl, when the curtain goes up, I latch on to the only little girl onstage. Wendy Moira Angela Darling—sister of Michael and

John, "mother" of the lost boys, and would-be "wife" of Peter Pan—is just like me. Well, except she has golden curls and a lilting soprano, and I have a frizzy Jew-fro, Coke-bottle glasses, and a freaked-out grandma. So actually, no, Wendy is nothing like me. But she's the girl I want to be. Pretty and perfect. Peter and the boys all love her so much they even sing a song about her: *"Oh what joy she'll bring to us! Make us pockets and sing to us."* I want to bring joy and make pockets. I want to be that kind of loved.

But Wendy isn't the only girl up on that stage. Another female is hiding in full drag. Wearing green tights and a belted tunic, the leader of the lost boys is played by a grown woman. Little me doesn't know it yet, but the message I'll take home from the Valley Music Theatre that day is this: You can act like a girl, sew pockets, and sing pretty. Or you can put your hands on your hips, crow like a rooster, and lead all the boys to amazing adventure.

CROSS-FADE (that's a TV term that means we're changing the scene now, moving forward in time): It's twenty-five years later. I am in the writers' room of *Cheers*, the Emmy Award–winning, top-rated show on TV. The action is set in a Boston sports bar "where everybody knows your name." Like a lot of sports bars, *Cheers* is a benevolent boys' club. And so is the *Cheers* writers' room, a rotating brotherhood of comedic geniuses distinguished by their shared love of foosball, Cuban cigars, and Chinese take-out served with whiskey. Then there's me, the female writer in the room, distinguished by a new baby at my breast and an age-old drive to keep all these playful boys on task so I can get my baby home to her crib before midnight.

Being the Wendy, the de facto mom, in the writers' room is a mixed bag. On the upside, you're not expected to be as funny as the guys. On the down-side, they rarely notice when you are. More often than not, I'll pitch a joke and get . . . crickets. My words evaporate into thin air as if I didn't speak them. I think, *Did I say that out loud or just think it to myself?* I learn to whisper my best pitches to the closest funny guy. Because when he repeats my joke, boom!

The joke gets heard, it goes into the script, and we're one joke closer to getting home by midnight.

In TV, writers grow up to become producers, and producers grow up to become executive producers, aka show-runners. This is where I go from being Wendy to Peter Pan; from being a girl among boys to a leader of men; from being the Joke Whisperer to the Show-runner.

The show-runner is responsible for . . . pretty much everything the light touches. On any given day, I live in the past (editing the episode we shot last week), in the future (prepping the episode we'll shoot next week), and in the constantly challenging present (rehearsing, revising, and extinguishing fires on the episode we're shooting this week). As *Cheers*'s first, and only, female show-runner, I do all that stuff . . . and push the show to number one. While nursing my newborn baby, backward and in high heels.

Not all the boys want to be led by a girl. No matter how the ratings soar, no matter how many awards roll in, no matter how early I get us home—I still manage to piss people off in a way that my male colleagues do not. I'm called "A" words like *abrasive* and *annoying* to my face. Behind my back, I am called "B" and "C" words I won't repeat. I am told to "shut up," "play nice," and "ride the horse in the direction it's going." I respond, "Yeah, but who stops the horse if it's going off a cliff?" I am told, "Honey, you've got to stop caring so much."

I try to stop caring. Not caring is not easy. So I stifle my caring until I can sneak off to the back lot, hide behind the fake New York deli facade, and cry it out. One February, I cry every day. Luckily February is a short month. Come March, I get back up on that horse, grab the reins, and ride it the direction it's going—until I need it to go a different way. Sorry, boys, that's just how I am. And how I want my daughters to grow up.

The guys in the writers' room nicknamed our firstborn daughter, Kit, *Cheers Baby*, and today our story comes full circle, with a neat ending that I did not see coming:

AS *CHEERS*'S FIRST,

AND ONLY,

FEMALE

SHOW-RUNNER, I DO
ALL THAT STUFF . . .

AND PUSH

THE SHOW TO

NUMBER ONE.

When I finished writing this draft, I Googled *gender fluid* and *Peter Pan*, just to see if anyone else had made that connection. To my humbled surprise, there were 606,000 results. To my even greater surprise, the very first one was a link to an article titled "Why Peter Pan Matters Today." I clicked it, and swear to Google, it was written in 2014 for a website called HelloGiggles by none other than . . . my *Cheers* baby, Kit Steinkellner!

Because *we* are girls, and storytellers, and pocket-makers, and tribe leaders, I can now see that I wasn't in my position of leadership just to win the awards, make the big bucks, and play with the boys. I was there to walk the walk for our *Cheers* baby, who grew up to become a writer herself. In fact, the week that I wrote this story, we saw the debut of *her* first TV show—all about another woman writer named Zelda Fitzgerald. And Kit wrote it in a room full of women.

Photo credit: Elisabeth McKay/ McKayImaging

BRENDA BOWEN

My father belonged to the Royal Automobile Club in London when I was a girl. He was one of its more unlikely members. A former WWII navy pilot who grew up in rural New Jersey, he sported a crew cut and spoke with an American accent rather than the plummy Oxbridge tones favored in those gilded rooms. On Sundays, RAC members were permitted to bring their families to eat in the Moorish dining room or swim in the Grecian pool. (During the week, the men bathed there naked.) One lucky Sunday, when I was not quite eleven, I was the family member who got to go.

In my bedroom, watched over by my posters of Mike Nesmith and Marc Bolan, I rolled up my sensible black one-piece bathing suit in a checkered towel, found my swim cap, and put them in a bag for my dad to carry. I planned to dress up for the occasion, and I refused to be burdened with a plain old canvas shopping bag. My oldest sister (the future college professor) was featuring bohemian styles at the time—

embroidered coats, peasant blouses. My second sister (the future union president) favored a uniform of orange pants and an earth-toned brown shirt, which she wore almost every single day.

But for me, ten years old in the spring of 1970, dressing up for the RAC meant wearing my go-to trendy ensemble of the season: tomato-red bell-bottom pants and thigh-length matching vest, coupled with a psychedelic blouse, and finished with white patent leather shoes with large silver buckles. (Note that the buttons on the vest were also silver.)

I rocked that look.

Dad and I drove up to London, found a parking space on a street off Pall Mall, and hand in hand, sauntered up to the entrance of the club. When we arrived at the imposing stone edifice, which looks not unlike Buckingham Palace, I flashed a big grin at the uniformed doorman and followed my father through the polished door. Our arrival, which should not have caused a stir, did. The club manager glided swiftly over to us and stopped my father with the hushed words, "I'm sorry, sir. We have a strict no-trouser rule for ladies."

A strict no-trouser rule for ladies. *Of ten.*

Women have been told how to dress since they could walk upright. Shirts can't be too tight. Or too loose—I recently discovered that in eighteenth-century Paris, a *loose* dress signaled sexual availability. Skirts cannot, of course, be too high. Or too low. Nor can heels. Heads must be covered. Heads must be uncovered. Heads must be bowed. Even as I write this, a controversy is swirling about two young girls barred from air travel because their pants were not the "right" pants. As you read this, there will likely be another.

My father, fighting mad, led me out of the club. "That's not a good rule," he said. "Let's get you a dress."

"How about if I take my pants off?" I countered.

This, we both agreed, was a superb idea. We would comply with their bad rule by subverting it. Plus, I'd get to wear a micro-miniskirt. We walked back to

WOMEN HAVE BEEN TOLD
HOW TO DRESS SINCE THEY COULD
WALK UPRIGHT.
SHIRTS CAN'T BE TOO TIGHT.
OR TOO LOOSE. . . .
SKIRTS CANNOT, OF COURSE,
BE TOO HIGH. OR TOO LOW. NOR
CAN HEELS. HEADS MUST BE
COVERED. HEADS MUST BE
UNCOVERED.
HEADS MUST BE
BOWED.

WOMEN OF MY ERA HAVE BECOME
EXPERT AT FINDING WAYS
AROUND BAD RULES:
THE ONES THAT SAY WE GET PAID
LESS THAN MEN,
THAT OUR WORK IS
NOT AS VALUED,
THAT WE DON'T KNOW
HOW TO GOVERN
OUR OWN THOUGHTS
OR BODIES.

the car, I slipped into the backseat, and with my father acting as guard, I shimmied out of my pants and emerged in my vest, compliant with the no-trouser rule. We walked back to the club and were granted immediate admittance, and I had my swim in the pool. There were no naked men.

The moral of this story is not that it's time to stop making rules about how women dress. That we already know.

The moral of this story is that—at ten years old—I was already good at the work-around, because I was a girl. Women of my era have become expert at finding ways around bad rules: the ones that say we get paid less than men, that our work is not as valued, that we don't know how to govern our own thoughts or bodies. As girls, we took in very early that we needed to resort to the work-around if we were to be granted access as equals. Or to be granted access at all.

ARTISTIC DIRECTOR OF THE
WASHINGTON NATIONAL OPERA AND
ARTISTIC AND GENERAL DIRECTOR
OF THE GLIMMERGLASS FESTIVAL
Photo credit: Stephen Voss Photography

FRANCESCA ZAMBELLO

I have spent forty years working in the theater. Not in front of the curtain on the side of the footlights but on the other side.

My mother was an actress and used to take me to the theater when she was performing, and I would sleep in her dressing room some nights while she was onstage. I became fascinated at an early age with the backstage world, the moving scenery, the fast costume changes, the colored lights . . . everything that it took to make the show. I could sit and watch rehearsals from the side for hours by the time I was five. I wasn't interested in performing; no, I wanted to *make* the stories.

By the time I was in third grade, I was creating shows with puppets under our grand piano. That safe space beneath the dark wooden sounding board was like a little theater proscenium for me. I would tape curtains to the front curve of the piano and add a theatrical drop that I had painted in the backyard. Then I would hide behind it and stick out my hands with the puppets on them. I became obsessed with making up stories and presenting them in my piano theater. The good thing was, no one told me a girl couldn't be the director! That would come later.

When I was growing up, my family moved to Europe, first to Paris and then Vienna. In these amazing capital cities, I would often spend time sitting in cafés, where I became a compulsive people-watcher, which led to my creating characters in my mind and making up stories. All I wanted to do as I grew up was to tell stories through images, music, and words.

After college, I moved to New York City with every intention of becoming a director. Friends were not very positive about this idea. Women worked in the theater, sure, but not as the number one creative person and leader of a show. There were no role models I could easily draw upon. So I set out to work my way up, first as a production assistant (read: coffee-getter), then as a stage manager. A director took a chance on me and hired me as his assistant, and eventually I started directing in very small places. When I tell it like this, it sounds easy. It wasn't—it was hard. There were lots of other people in line, lots of men and guys with special connections. The best thing I did was leave New York and look elsewhere for work. I found directing jobs in Europe and less obvious places like Milwaukee! Over time, I built a résumé and a solid career away from the big US cities.

A story that has always stayed with me is from the Vienna State Opera, one of the most prestigious companies in the world. The general director called my agent and invited me to come direct there. This was a huge coup, and my agent called back and said yes on my behalf. Suddenly it came to light that the general director had invited *Francesco* (the male version of my name), not *Francesca*. A woman had *never* directed in Vienna, and he said one never would. He withdrew the offer, saying it had been a mistake. (A woman finally made it there a few years back, but I never did.)

Flash-forward to now. I have often been alone on many frontiers in my field

I WASN'T INTERESTED IN PERFORMING; NO, I WANTED TO *MAKE* THE STORIES.

THE GOOD THING WAS,
NO ONE
TOLD ME A GIRL
COULDN'T
BE THE DIRECTOR!
THAT WOULD
COME LATER.

as a female director in opera and theater, and sometimes even more alone in the last decade as the artistic director of two opera companies. I have now directed in more than two hundred theaters and opera houses around the world, on stages in locations as diverse as the jungle of Cambodia, Disneyland, and Broadway. I truly believe I often had to work harder to pass my male colleagues. It is not always a happy ending, but for me there was a truth to hard work and creative talent and a fair amount of self-belief in many dark moments!

Now I devote considerable energy to supporting my female colleagues as they come into the field. We are still a vast minority, but we're gaining. And, of course, there is the *logic* to it all: Women make up half the audience, so why shouldn't half the people who create the images and tell the stories be women?

BABETTE DAVIS

"A closed mouth doesn't get fed." This was one of my momma's many adages. She would say it on a regular basis in an effort to get me to speak. But she would also say, "Stay in a child's place." What a contradiction! I learned at an early age that the best way to stay in my place was to keep my mouth shut. Although I wasn't even sure what my place was since my mom had boarded me out to someone whom I refer to as my "wicked godmother"—and I didn't give her that title for fun. As an act of punishment, this woman made me wear pants to school on picture day—this was in the 1950s, and little girls always wore dresses on picture day. (She also used to make me sleep in the garage with her dog, Bugga Bear.) Wearing pants that day was the worst. I was the laughingstock of the school.

My childhood was full of contradictions. I grew up in South Los Angeles, with a black mother who was married to an Italian before the civil rights movement. My mother was a domestic worker, and her job required her to live with her employers, a Jewish family—that's why she left me in the care of my wicked godmother during the week. The way I saw it, my momma should have been taking care of her own child, not someone else's, but who was I to say anything? I was just a child staying in her place, a child with a closed mouth, looking to be fed.

On my eighth birthday, my momma held an amazing birthday party for me. I actually felt like a normal kid that day. I was the princess; all eyes were on me. My momma made me a candy cake with white frosting and bought me my first pair of white oxford shoes, with which I could wear a pair of fold-down, ruffled socks. I remember smiling all day long. The sun shined a little brighter on that day, and there was no need to keep my mouth shut. I ate until my heart was content.

When the party was over, so was my time with my momma. It was time for me to return to my godmother's. I gathered my belongings and watched my mother's husband load them into his car.

"Did you enjoy your day?" my momma asked.

I nodded and smiled.

"I can't hear a nod, Babette."

"Yes, Momma," I responded.

My mother ushered me to the car—she was staying home to clean up while her husband drove me to my godmother's house. I hugged her and got into the car. I was sitting on the floor in the backseat because there was no way I wanted anyone to see me in the car with an Italian. A colored girl and an Italian stepfather? Another contradiction.

On the way home, my mother's husband pulled into an empty parking lot and whispered, "I have one more surprise for you."

I hopped off the floor and with a burst of excitement asked, "What is it?"

He gestured for me to climb over the seat. "I promised you I'd teach you to drive, but your feet aren't long enough to reach the pedals. So here's the deal. We are going to work as a team. You sit in my lap and steer, and I will press the pedals for you."

Momma would have a fit if she knew, but who could pass up such an opportunity? I hurried to sit on his lap, and the escapade began. I was having a ball, and so was he, but at my expense. I knew something felt wrong, yet I was having so much fun—another contradiction.

That day was the beginning of a cycle of sexual abuse, and I remained silent—I stayed in a child's place. I eventually moved back home with my momma. The abuse continued for several years. It had become such a regular occurrence that I became accustomed to it. One day, my momma's husband followed me into a closet, and my little sister (whom he never abused in any capacity) witnessed it. She threatened to tell my mother. I'm not sure if she did, because my mother never had a conversation with me about it. But that was the last day he ever took advantage of my innocence. His abuse stopped that day!

My mother remained married to him well into my adulthood. My daughter even referred to him as grandpa, and I still remained silent. I tried very hard to block those memories, and I did this as a coping mechanism. I turned my pain into passion, and with every project I ventured into, I gave it one hundred percent. But I never addressed the abuse until I got older and had the opportunity to speak with a professional therapist.

I am now a successful business owner and motivational speaker, and as a chef, I not only encourage people to open their mouths and be fed nutritious food, but I also encourage people to be heard. There is a contradiction about silence. It can be an asset but also a hindrance. Any child who suffers from abuse should SHOUT, SCREAM, and KICK until she is not only heard but also fed the love she deserves.

There are many sentient beings, including animals, who suffer daily from abuse. Animals, unlike humans, have no choice but to remain silent because they can't speak. It is my desire to one day start an organization that supports both abused children and animals, one in which the kids and the animals help one another heal.

GRAMMY AWARD-WINNING
SONGWRITER AND PRODUCER
Photo credit: www.mattbeard.com/
Matt Beard Photography, Inc.

HOLLY KNIGHT

I came into this world with my creative spirit intact, no doubt about it. By the time I was four, I could play music by ear. I would listen to my mother practice piano, and when she walked out of the room, I'd sit down and play whatever she'd just played. I loved music so much I practiced before school, after school—any chance I could get—and where other parents forced their kids to practice, mine had to ask me to take a break.

When I was eight, I discovered rock music—the *louder* the better. From that point on, all I wanted was to be in a rock band.

Years later, when I was sixteen, with the dream still burning bright, I left home to chase it. When I told my mother I wasn't going to pursue a career in the classical world, she was devastated. She thought that I was throwing away ten years of hard work and that my talent would go to waste, that I would abandon music altogether, but I had other plans. I loved classical music, and I wasn't going to stop playing; I just wanted to do so much more.

Right away, I noticed that while many talented female singers were out there, hardly any were female *musicians*, certainly not in any of the rock bands I grew up listening to—Led Zeppelin, The Doors, The Stones, and The Beatles, and as I got older, Queen and Aerosmith. Even today, it's rare to see a female guitarist, drummer, or bass player, and usually when you do, you hear "She's really good . . . for a girl." How about just "she's really good"?

If men have anything over women, maybe it's their brute strength and ability to lift heavy things. But in music, to play any instrument skillfully, whether it's electric guitar, keyboards, or any other instrument (with the exception of drums . . . maybe), it takes no physical superiority at all. In fact, it's quite the opposite; to play well requires dexterity and fine motor skills and, of course, talent. The idea that only guys can rock and play brilliantly is ridiculous. So why do men have the monopoly on rock music?

Despite the lack of other female artists, I was not dissuaded from my dream. At age sixteen, I strutted into the man cave that is the music industry and never looked back. I helped to form my first band, Spider, in the late 1970s. I was the keyboardist, and one other woman was in the band—the singer. We were a hard rock band, and we kicked ass. After a year of playing and showcasing, we recorded a bunch of original songs and got signed to a record label. Without knowing who wrote what, the record label always picked the songs I wrote as the singles, and after two records, I left the band to pursue a full-time career writing songs for other artists and bands.

My career started moving incredibly fast, and I owe a ton of gratitude to Mike Chapman, my mentor, who took me under his wing. The first big hits I had as a songwriter were "Better Be Good to Me," an international smash for Tina Turner on her record *Private Dancer*, and "Love Is a Battlefield" for Pat Benatar, both of which I wrote with Mike. After that, I started to write hits on my own or with other collaborators, such as "The Warrior" for Patty Smyth and "Never" with Heart. These artists happened to be women, and I think they responded to my ethos of female empowerment. I was fierce and passionate, and they connected with that.

EVEN TODAY, IT'S RARE TO SEE A FEMALE GUITARIST, DRUMMER, OR BASS PLAYER, AND USUALLY WHEN YOU DO, YOU HEAR "SHE'S REALLY GOOD . . . FOR A GIRL." HOW ABOUT JUST "SHE'S REALLY GOOD"?

The real game changer came when I started writing for or with male rock bands and artists, like Aerosmith, Bon Jovi, and Rod Stewart. I was really the first woman to do that, and it was a lot of fun. I got along great with most of them. Then there were the times when I felt animosity and jealousy from the guys. The question "Why is an outside songwriter being brought in to write when we're all writers?" was asked on a number of occasions. And my silent thought would be, *Because, dummy, the label felt you weren't writing the hits . . . so deal with it.* To add insult to injury, the fact that the outside songwriter was a woman really emasculated them.

As my career took off, I started to produce a lot of my demo recordings, and that's when I really felt a pushback from the record companies and managers. Now that I'd established myself as a hit songwriter, everyone would take my calls. However, the minute I told them I wanted to produce the track, they'd shut down. (In music, a producer is in charge of getting the best performance out of the singers and musicians and arranging the music; in essence, the captain steering the ship.) Here it was again . . . only *men* could produce because it involved leadership skills and knowing how to deal with bands and musicians. How could a woman possibly do that?

By "accident," I was able to produce some of the recordings. For instance, I wrote two songs for *Thelma and Louise*. Director Ridley Scott loved the songs, as well as the way my recordings sounded. When he received new versions of my songs produced by a well-known producer, he said that if he couldn't use the original recording, he would remove them from the sound track. The beauty is, I doubt he cared who produced the tracks, he just liked my production, and that was very affirming for me. So it's not about whether you're a boy or a girl, or who you are, but whether you do the best job in the end. It's not always like that, but it should be.

Throughout my career, I'd face similar obstacles. There was always some male band member or executive who didn't take me seriously, whether I was brought in to write a song, play keyboards on a track (I had played keyboards on

Kiss's *Unmasked*), or produce the recording. But then I'd get down to business, and I could see a shift in their attitude and feel a level of respect that wasn't there before. They realized that I knew what I was talking about and that I was accomplished and successful for a reason. This happened most of the time, but not always.

Once, many years ago, an interviewer asked me why all my songs seemed to be about fighting, songs like "Love Is a Battlefield," "The Warrior," "Invincible," and "Stick to Your Guns." It was never a conscious choice; I just wrote what was real to me. The truth is, my songs were often about fighting *for* something, not fighting with someone. We all discover things worth fighting for . . . and as women, we have to fight that much harder.

I believe in women helping women. I believe in the next generation of young girls and pushing them to achieve their desires, whatever and wherever that may be. I love men, and the truly secure ones aren't intimidated by a strong, intelligent woman; in fact, they're turned on. As for the rest, they can go wait in the car—I got this.

So it's been a wild ride and a wonderful career, but I've had to be tough and tender at the same time. In 2013, I was inducted into the Songwriters Hall of Fame. At that time, there were over four hundred inductees, and only sixteen of them were women. I think being inducted was the moment I finally stopped looking for validation from others. I already knew what I had accomplished, and while I'm proud of the recognition, I didn't need a crystal statuette to tell me that my songs brought joy and happiness to people all over the world. The bottom line is, the only one you need validation from is yourself. Once you discover that, there's nothing you can't do.

THE 1960s

o   CONGRESS PASSES THE EQUAL PAY ACT, A FEDERAL LAW PROHIBITING
    SEXUAL DISCRIMINATION AS IT APPLIES TO COMPENSATION IN THE
    WORKPLACE, AND THE CIVIL RIGHTS ACT, WHICH FORBIDS DISCRIMINATION
    BASED ON RACE, COLOR, RELIGION, NATIONAL ORIGIN, AND SEX.

o   FEMALE WORKERS EARN ONLY AN AVERAGE OF 59 CENTS TO THE MALE
    WORKER'S DOLLAR.

o   THE NATIONAL ORGANIZATION FOR WOMEN IS CREATED TO
    MOBILIZE WOMEN BY PUTTING PRESSURE ON EMPLOYERS AND
    THE GOVERNMENT TO PROMOTE FULL EQUALITY OF MEN AND WOMEN.

o   HAWAII ELECTS PATSY TAKEMOTO MINK TO CONGRESS, WHERE SHE SERVES
    AS THE FIRST WOMAN OF COLOR IN THE HOUSE OF REPRESENTATIVES.

o   RACHEL CARSON PUBLISHES *SILENT SPRING*, A BOOK DOCUMENTING
    THE DETRIMENTAL EFFECTS OF THE WIDESPREAD USE OF PESTICIDES,
    WHICH SPURS A MAJOR ENVIRONMENTAL MOVEMENT AND LEADS TO
    THE CREATION OF THE ENVIRONMENTAL PROTECTION AGENCY.

o   TO PROTEST UNFAIR WORKING CONDITIONS, DOLORES HUERTA
    COFOUNDS THE NATIONAL FARM WORKERS ASSOCIATION, WHICH
    WILL BECOME THE UNITED FARM WORKERS, WITH CESAR CHAVEZ. IT
    PROVIDES THOUSANDS OF LEADERSHIP OPPORTUNITIES TO WOMEN,
    INCLUDING JESSIE LOPEZ DE LA CRUZ, ONE OF THE UNION'S FIRST
    FEMALE ORGANIZERS WORKING IN THE FIELDS.

MARGARET STOHL

For sixteen years, I was a writer and designer of video games in various buildings mostly full of men. I thought of them collectively as *Boyland*— the straight, white, gamer bros who owned the industry, top to bottom. There were some women here and there, but not often in production; they were in sales or in marketing or in communications. One studio I briefly freelanced for openly made it a point never to hire any women full time; Boyland thought it was too distracting. Women were never designers or artists or programmers or staff writers. Occasionally, they would become producers, but sometimes even after that happened, Boyland would drive them away, as they did to my friend J. She still brings it up when I see her now, sometimes.

The exceptions were notable. Once, a woman was the director of my project. She was tiny and fierce and wandered around the office wrapped in a blanket late at night, giving orders to Boyland and ignoring it when they paid her back by getting drunk and leaving death threats on her answering machine. It was a joke, they said. She didn't think it was all that funny.

That director eventually left, but a few years later, another woman became my boss. Boyland got rid of her, too, but not until after she'd ordered the place to put free tampons in all the bathrooms, so I didn't have to slink there with one hidden up my sleeve. I remembered thinking it was the most radical act I'd ever witnessed. When she left, I gave her a silver bracelet with a lock on it and wrote a note about her newfound freedom. But we both knew it wasn't exactly that. She had become too powerful and had been exiled. That was my take, anyway; that was what happened to girls in Boyland. We had to be careful. We had to learn to cuss like sailors and dress like guys. We had to avoid girly clothes and hide our boobs and not wear pink, unless it was ironic. We had to be able to talk about science fiction and watch war movies. I still do.

Twenty-five years ago, the women's bathroom was my personal office because I was the only woman on the floor, at least to my knowledge. I kept things there and joked that I should move my desk. There were plenty of jokes, and Boyland's jokes were worse than mine. Once, I walked into a room for a meeting I was leading. A programmer friend of mine glanced up and said, "Oh look, the stripper's here." People laughed. Maybe I laughed, too, I can't remember. I probably didn't say anything at all. I wanted to be invited to lunch, and to be invited to lunch you had to be one of the guys.

In Boyland, you had to learn to take a joke, even if that meant being called a stripper. Even if it meant hearing that you were "smoking hot" and that it was a distraction. Even if it meant being told you should get a "chastity belt" because you were spending too much time with the boys on the team.

I moved to a different studio not long after that one. I guess I didn't think it was all that funny, either. I also didn't think it was funny when I got a photo of my own house mailed to me, with a threatening letter. Or even now, when I get death threats online. Sometimes it can be exhausting to have a sense of humor in Boyland.

After sixteen years in the video game industry—as a writer, a designer, a consultant, a creative director, and ultimately a studio cofounder and co-owner—I left. I began writing YA novels and, as a result, began working with writers, editors, publicists, librarians, teachers, marketing executives, and publishers who were almost all women. It was liberating and thrilling. My husband retired and became, for the time being, a stay-at-home dad. Many of my close female friends were writers who supported their own families. Some had come from journalism, some from politics, some from the tech industry. We commiserate over the crap we've been through, and the crap we won't go through now. We write strong female characters. We have daughters. We hope for better. We hope for more. We tell ourselves that times have changed, that they'll keep changing. Then we hope it's true.

My oldest daughter graduated from Columbia University with a degree in computer science and statistics in 2016. She's smart and strategic and knows more about video games than most of the boys in Boyland. And yet, when she applied for game-programming jobs last spring, I was surprised to hear one of her first interview questions: *Why aren't you going into sales or marketing? You shouldn't feel like you have to be a rocket scientist. . . .* She went on to find a job at an e-sports company. She knows Boyland as well as I do.

We are two generations of girls in Boyland, my daughter and I, though I am no longer young enough to be called a girl, and the industry is increasingly no longer young enough to openly remain a Boyland. Our progress is subtle, but that doesn't mean it's not real. I still sometimes work as a consultant for video game companies, but only on my terms, and only when I want to. I also write YA, and now comics; I write a girl superhero series for Marvel—*Mighty Captain Marvel*—where my editor is a woman, Sana Amanat. She is also the head of Content and Character Development, which makes her pretty much the Boss of Boyland. We still both get death threats from trolls. When we go to the Marvel Creative Summits, we are sometimes still the only girls in the room. I still dress like a boy and swear like a pirate.

But do you know what the difference is? Now we have ways to reach out and talk about Boyland, not just with one another but with younger women,

NOW WE HAVE VOICES. NOW WE HAVE PLATFORMS. NOW WE HAVE ALLIES. NOW WE HAVE ONE ANOTHER. NOW WE FIGHT.

too. Now we openly talk about advocacy groups, representation, and mentoring. Now we track the crappy hiring statistics in Silicon Valley. Now we teach girls to program. Now we call our local and national representatives. Now we march on Washington and across the world. Now we have voices. Now we have platforms. Now we have allies. Now we have one another. Now we fight.

Now Rey has a lightsaber. Now Captain Marvel has a movie. Now the Black Widow appears in toy lines. Now the Force is with us. How long will I still have to wait for my Girl Dumbledore and Girl Yoda and Girl Gandalf?

We won't wait much longer. At least, our daughters won't. We've made sure of that much. The attack on Boyland has finally begun.

ANNA PONDER

In the Sterling Memorial Library at Yale, there is a portrait of Edward A. Bouchet, the first black American to earn a PhD at a US institution. As a PhD student, I would smile as I passed it—proud to be part of such a meaningful tradition.

Most of the challenges in my life have been framed by racial identity. I grew up in Columbia, South Carolina. In 1976, my older sister was the first black high school student from South Carolina to serve as a page in the US Senate. I was the second in 1981. She was the first black student to graduate from Heathwood Hall, a respected private school. I was the fifth. And, as I stood with my classmates on the steps of Trinity Episcopal Cathedral for a photo, we faced the capitol, where the Confederate flag waved atop the dome.

When I enrolled in Yale's PhD program in political science in September 1992, I found myself part of another meaningful tradition— brilliantly marked by *The Women's Table*, a Maya Lin sculpture installed in front of Sterling in 1993. Although women had matriculated at the School of Fine Arts as well as certain graduate and professional programs since the 1860s, Yale College graduated its first truly coeducational class in 1971. Twenty years later, I discovered a university culture that thought surprisingly little about my race but quite a lot about my gender. Female students, faculty, staff, and administrators were few and remained "others." There were no female faculty members in the political science department when I arrived.

In my first year, a professor decided to share "anonymous" examples of poorly written and/or poorly conceived work by reading excerpts from three papers aloud in class. Mine was one—along with those of the two other women in the room. I think I shocked him when I spoke up to claim the work (my classmates had not) and asked pointed questions about what he would have preferred. The following day he left a gift in my cubby—a copy of Strunk and White's *The Elements of Style*. I took it with me to his office, where I sat down and said that I would like to go through my paper (which he had failed to mark up with any commentary) in tedious detail. My thought: If you're going to go out of your way to embarrass me, let's make the most of it. And, of course, a bully is typically uncomfortable with any confrontation but his own. Trying to bring our tutorial to an end, he suggested that I "may not have what it takes to be successful in the program." I looked at him and said that there were only two ways out for me: "with a degree or in a pine box." Then gathering my things, I added: "See you at the finish line."

I graduated in 1998 and, funnily enough, seldom—if ever—use the title "Dr." Frankly, I prefer to be called Anna, and Ms. is also just fine with me. That said, when I made a career move into hedge funds in 2006, I put "Anna Ponder, PhD" on my business cards—admittedly because in this testosterone-driven business, women are often undervalued. Nearly two years into my tenure, my group spun off to form an independent firm, wherein I was the only woman outside the assistants' pool. As we went through branding for the new company, the new

. . . HE SUGGESTED THAT I "MAY NOT HAVE WHAT IT TAKES TO BE SUCCESSFUL IN THE PROGRAM." I LOOKED AT HIM AND SAID THAT THERE WERE ONLY TWO WAYS OUT FOR ME: "WITH A DEGREE OR IN A PINE BOX."

"IF YOU ARE NOT 'MISSUS,' WHAT TITLE WOULD YOU POSSIBLY USE?" BEWILDERMENT SPREAD TO MY FACE AS I RESPONDED: "DOCTOR?"

senior managing director, who had not been with us at the old firm, caught sight of my card. When he appeared at my office door to speak with me about it, he said I should remove the PhD "because it makes the guys uncomfortable."

I made no change to my business card.

Not long after, I was out with an old friend, who was in town with her mother. After a wonderful dinner talking, laughing, and generally catching up, "Mrs. X" asked for my email so we could keep in touch. I gave her my business card. She looked at it and said, somewhat in horror, "PhD on your card? My God . . . you'll never get a man." I thought, but out of politeness did not say: *You may be right, but how happy could I be with a man who would reject me out of hand because of my education?*

One last piece to this evolving life puzzle. My parents have been and remain my biggest advocates. Both are academics and hold doctoral degrees. As I walked across the stage to receive my Yale diploma, I looked out to find them in the audience. I saw my mother but not my dad. I turned my head back toward the stairway to descend from the stage, and there he was at the bottom, arms out-stretched, and smiling with his whole heart. I ran down to meet him. He hugged me and said how proud he was. It was a magical moment, which I cherish.

I have always thought that it is wonderful that my father, who was reared "old school," had daughters. He invested every bit of paternal hope and ambition in us. But there were a few bumps along the way. He once asked whether I might marry a man I was dating seriously while in graduate school. I said perhaps, and we continued talking about what that life might look like. In the course of the discussion, I told him I doubted that I would ever change my name. I said that I like my name because it is part of my family—my history. I treasure the legacy. He looked at me bewildered and asked, "If you are not 'missus,' what title would you possibly use?" Bewilderment spread to my face as I responded: "Doctor?" That discussion reverberates to this day with my father's pride in my choices and in my thinking. I hear it and feel it every time he smiles and calls me "Doctor Ponder."

JILL LORIE

As a little girl, I did all the things that were expected of little girls of the time: baking cookies, taking dance classes, playing with Barbies. I didn't particularly enjoy any of these activities; it was just what girls did. Because I was a girl, it wasn't "right" for me to build traps, jump off roofs, clown around, or play baseball, even though I wanted to do all those things and had the ability to do them. Instead, as I'd been taught, I intentionally missed a ground ball, pretended the boys were rude, and stopped myself from interjecting all the superfunny things I had to say.

In high school, I learned that gossip, makeup, and popularity were the keys to success and devoted myself to being successful. I did just well enough in my classes to keep my parents and teachers off my back and to retain an appearance of cool. I would erase my calculus homework and pretend I didn't understand the math so I could be tutored by the cute senior boys. And I got away with a lot using some tried-and-true tactics. I'd don a sad face to be excused from missed homework assignments. Flirty smiles would get me out of tardies. Mediocrity and feigned helplessness never felt right, but in high school, that is what I thought being a girl was all about.

I showed up at college with no goals other than to get out of my parents' house and to have fun. But the cool girls were far different from any I'd encountered—they didn't shave their legs, and they discussed literature and politics. As in my youth, I was most interested in being popular, so I spent the next four years trying to fit in with them and failing miserably. I couldn't force myself to care about the things they cared about.

I coasted through college with no real sense of myself, no idea of my potential, and no idea of who I wanted to be. At the advice of my father, I majored in English and got my degree in education. But I had no real desire to be a teacher. Instead, I spent my early twenties as a "groupie," a groupie who earned peanuts working for a rock 'n' roll legend. I budgeted tours, licensed the catalog, negotiated publishing rights, threw record-release parties, and scheduled video shoots. I did all this while coordinating travel so the wives and girlfriends never ran into each other on the road. I loved the work, and for the first time in my life, I felt capable and in control—feelings I never realized I so eagerly craved. Still, for all my hard work and success, I was treated and paid like a girl who just wanted to hang out with the band.

When the musician refused to pay me more, I quit. I felt emboldened and decided to put my college degree to use. I was lucky to land a teaching position in Covina, California. It was summer, and the job started in the fall. To bridge the gap, I accepted a six-week temp job at JPMorgan Chase. That summer at the bank was my awakening. In six weeks, I went from being the temp receptionist to the manager's assistant to someone who was managing her own book of business. For me, the metamorphosis was the window to my potential. I suddenly saw myself as a smart girl with possibilities.

By the following September, I had brought in over $100 million in business.

FOR ME, THE METAMORPHOSIS WAS THE WINDOW TO MY POTENTIAL. I SUDDENLY SAW MYSELF AS A SMART GIRL WITH POSSIBILITIES.

I LET GO OF MY PRECONCEIVED NOTIONS OF WHAT A GIRL WAS **ALLOWED** TO DO AND BE. I SHAVED MY LEGS AND TOOK CARE WITH MY HAIR AND MAKEUP *AND* PLAYED FANTASY FOOTBALL WITH THE GUYS.

I'd spent years living up to others' (low) expectations of me. But no longer. I let go of my preconceived notions of what a girl was allowed to do and be. I shaved my legs and took care with my hair and makeup *and* played fantasy football with the guys. I joked with my male colleagues and wore cocktail dresses to work, all the while closing more deals—and harder deals—than any man in the office. I found success being a woman who is comfortable being a girl and who is confident in her abilities.

KATRINA ADAMS

I fell in love with tennis the first time I hit a ball. I loved the feel of the ball on the racquet. I loved being in control of my own shots. I loved that you didn't have anyone but yourself to rely on. It's up to you how you train and practice to get better. Your destiny on the court is entirely in your own hands.

I would go on to play professional tennis and win twenty Women's Tennis Association doubles titles and compete in dozens of Grand Slam tournaments. I played from Melbourne to Russia and everywhere in between. I am now the president of the United States Tennis Association. Tennis opened up the world for me.

But it almost never happened.

I started playing tennis kind of by accident. When I was six years old, in 1975, I attended a summer program run by the Dr. Martin Luther King Jr. Boys Club on Chicago's West Side. (The clubs were later renamed the Boys & Girls Clubs of America because several girls also attended and participated in club activities.) My older brothers were part of the program, which was for kids between nine and eighteen years old.

My parents were public-school teachers and taught summer school, so I had to tag along with my brothers. This left me on the side, watching them and the other kids practice. I had a great deal of confidence that I could not only play as well as they could but that I could beat them. So every day, I begged the coaches to allow me to play. They finally gave in and decided to give me a chance. By the end of the program, I was named the Most Improved Player of the entire summer.

Don't forget: All the other campers were older than I was and had six weeks to practice. I had only four.

Though I loved tennis, I never thought of playing the sport as a profession. My parents were teachers, so that's what I initially aspired to be. Somewhere along the way, I thought I would become an accountant (even though I didn't like math). I didn't choose tennis as a pathway until my middle teens, when I became the Illinois High School Association singles champion. Eventually, I earned a scholarship to Northwestern University, where I won the National Collegiate Athletic Association's doubles championship. And from there, I started competing professionally.

Not everyone is able to find success out on the tour coming from my background. I was one of fewer than a dozen African-American tennis players at the professional level during my tenure. I felt pressure to represent my family, the kids I grew up training with in Chicago, my community, my entire race.

I owe a lot to tennis; I found myself on the court. Tennis allows you to be your true self. Your personality emerges from your style of play and how you act on the court. I have an assertive personality and a *gung ho* attitude—those traits translated into an aggressive game. Unlike other girls who were told to be sweeter and calmer and more reserved, I was encouraged to wear my emotions on my sleeve and show my passion. I learned to be proud of who I am and work my hardest every single day on the court and, eventually, in the boardroom.

I also owe just as much to the people who helped me achieve my dreams. A village truly does raise a child—and I had a tennis village to raise me. When I first started, I was the youngest in my group. The other girls were teenagers—I looked up to them as big sisters. Though my brothers only played that one summer, they became my biggest fans and would end up driving me to many practices.

My parents also supported me every step of the way. I didn't understand until I was older how much my parents had sacrificed to support my path as a tennis player, but they did what was necessary to make sure I had the opportunities provided for me to be the best that I could be. When my parents weren't able to take me to tournaments, Helyn Edwards, a woman who competed on the pro circuit, practiced with me and made sure I could get to my matches. I am so grateful to her.

When I retired from playing tennis, I turned to a life of service. I went straight into being a national coach. I was one of two African-American coaches at that time and one of three female coaches, but I was highly respected because of my success as a player and the way I communicated and worked with the players. They looked up to me, both the boys and the girls. At the end of the day, when you're a professional player, you're your own boss. My responsibilities were so much greater when I became a coach because nothing was about me. It was all about someone else.

As the president of the United States Tennis Association and only the fourth woman in this role, I'm always trying to figure out how to support others, especially our younger players and those who come from backgrounds that may not be as familiar with tennis, especially within the Hispanic community. In addition, I focus on making sure women have leadership roles in the association. It's vital to continue to diversify the image of our sport. On all levels and in all categories. People tend to think that the USTA wants to get everyone involved in tennis to be a professional player, but that's not the case. We want people to get into the sport for the pure sake of the sport and for the health benefits of being active. It's the sport of a lifetime. People from five to ninety-five years old are playing tennis. It's a sport *for* a lifetime.

UNLIKE OTHER GIRLS WHO WERE TOLD TO BE SWEETER AND CALMER AND MORE RESERVED, WAS ENCOURAGED TO WEAR MY EMOTIONS ON MY SLEEVE AND SHOW MY PASSION.

Whenever I speak to young players, I tell them to embrace the path that they lead. We're all put on certain paths whether we choose them or not. There's always going to be a journey. There's no easy way to the top. There are always going to be challenges.

Enjoy the battle.

LIBBA BRAY

They told me my anger was a thing with teeth, a dangerous beast that could maim and kill if I were reckless enough to let it out. They told me my anger was ugly. Frightening. That it would make other people uncomfortable. That it made me unlovable.

"It's best to get along, to make everybody happy," they said.

"Don't be so sensitive. They were only joking," they said.

"Boys won't like you. Don't you want boys to like you?" they said.

"Smile," they said.

Show your teeth but not your bite.

Here is who told me this: The mothers and grandmothers, church ladies and crossing guards. Teachers. Politicians. Ministers. Boys. Girls. Comedians. Strangers on the street. Movies and TV, advertisements and cartoons. Soap operas. Magazines. Books. Song lyrics. Sometimes they said it outright. Other times, it was said through pinched mouths and narrowed eyes. Through sighs and long, judging silences. Through rolled eyes and teasing. Through the withdrawal of their love until I could smile and make them happy again. Sometimes they even told me in ways that made it seem like a kindness.

"You can catch more flies with honey than with vinegar," they said.

But why would I want a bunch of dead flies in the first place?

"This is for your own good," they said. "After all, you don't want anyone to think you're angry."

But I am angry!

"No, you're not," they'd say with assurance. "You might just be getting sick."

Here is what they meant by "angry": Having strong opinions. Objecting to being mistreated. Disagreeing without apology. Raising my voice. Saying no.

They told me all this until I was worn down. Until I no longer trusted any of my feelings. Until I no longer trusted myself.

Sometimes, I glimpsed a stiff-bristled tail flick out around the edges of the mothers and grandmothers and crossing guards telling me to keep my anger hidden. A hint of their own feral anger muzzled deep within. I could sense it the way one can feel the heat coming off the eye of a stove that someone has forgotten to turn off. I'd even seen them explode when they could take the pretending no more. I watched in awe as they breathed fire like glorious, beautiful dragons. But the people rolled their eyes. Shamed them. Shunned them. They hurled words like stones to bring the dragons down: "Hysterical." "Irrational." "Hormonal." "Ornery." "Nag." "Impossible." "Bitch."

"One of those angry women."

Some other woman would grab hold of the angry one then. "C'mon now, honey. You don't really mean that," she'd say with a smile, words like a leash around the dragon's neck.

She was only passing along the message she'd gotten from her mother, who'd gotten it from her mother, who'd gotten it from . . . well, you get the picture.

I watched it all, absorbed it like a punch. I began to equate anger with shame. With not being feminine. With being wrong. My anger was not a righteous truth-teller, a barometer of who to trust and who was an asshole. No. It was unseemly. It could make people not like me, which was clearly the very worst curse a girl could bring upon herself.

Now I, too, was afraid of what lived inside me. The sooner I locked it up, the better. Down in the basement of my soul, I held the leash of my anger and plucked the teeth from its mouth as it looked at me with sorrowful, betrayed eyes: *Why are you doing this to me? To us?* "It's for our own good," I parroted. My belly hurt like I'd swallowed boiling eels. "I can't let you out; it's too dangerous," I said as I latched the basement door. "Because we are a girl. And girls should not be angry."

Once upon a time, when my anger had no muzzle, I howled for three hours straight. I don't remember the particular injustice. I only know that I was outraged and wounded as only a four-year-old in full possession of herself can be. My rage was full-throated. Stiff-fisted. Tight-legged and arch-backed. Punk AF. People from all over the neighborhood came to watch the spectacle of my fury as I threw myself onto our front lawn and yelped my indignation even after I'd long run out of gas and was going on pure fumes.

"You still at it?" Mrs. Celeski said on her way to get her mail late in the afternoon. Her sons were off at war. She drank whiskey and cursed with abandon. She was the angriest person I knew, and even she did not like the thing growing inside me. "Don't you think you oughta quit by now?"

I did want to quit. I wanted to go inside. Eat a peanut butter and jelly sandwich. Drink some Kool-Aid. But I had not yet been heard. I just needed *someone* to hear me. My rage was impotent. Worse, it had made me an object of ridicule and scorn. Like so many girls before me.

When you're a girl, they expect you to numb what you really feel. What you know. They expect you to ignore that ache of angry truth creeping up the back of your throat while you try to swallow it down. They expect you to gaslight yourself. And after a while, you begin to question all your feelings. *Maybe I'm wrong? I must be wrong.* You hear yourself say things like:

"I mean, I'm not mad or anything."

"I hope this doesn't make me sound like a bitch."

. . . GET ANGRY.
DON'T DIE A
MARTYR
FOR THEIR
COMFORT.

"Oh, sure, I know it was just a joke."

"No, it's fine. I'm fine. Everything's fine."

"Sorry." "Sorry." "Sorry." "Sorry."

You forget how to howl. You forget that your feelings matter. You forget how to snarl along the fence: *Stand back or I swear I will come for you. This is your only warning.*

By high school, I had internalized the lessons well. I made friends with the angriest girls I could. I let them carry the water of my unbearable emotion. I hung behind as they stood out front, shouting truth to power, biting back—snap, snap, snap—taking their lumps. I envied them, of course. The girls who didn't pretend to feel anything other than what was real. Who called bullshit with deuces raised.

My own beast did not go away. Captivity made it shrewd. With no teeth in the way, its tongue grew large and clever-bladed. Why throw a direct punch when you could slip a shiv of sarcasm between the ribs, one-handed and unobserved, served with the polite smile they'd taught you was acceptable? *I was only joking—can't you take a joke?*

My hands ached from holding my own leash. My beast gnawed me from the inside, drawing blood. Better to bleed on the inside, I thought, than to let the thing out where everyone could see its ugliness. Occasionally, it got out anyway. It nosed the latch out of place to stand in the light of the kitchen. I laughed at it—"Oh that? That's just a joke!"—and it slunk back down the steps, stung by my smile.

Oh, I was a good daughter. A sweet girl. So very likable. I burned in silence.

One day, I was in an accident. A terrible accident. A slick spot in the road, a mangled car, and a mangled face. I was so broken that all the latches inside me came undone. No one wanted to look at me, at my scars, my new ugliness. No one wanted to hear my pain, so much pain. God, the pain.

"You're so strong. You just have to go on being strong," they said with a pat on the shoulder and those same narrowed eyes. They did not care if I choked to death on my razor-blade feelings as long as I did not make them uncomfortable. As long as I didn't howl with rage and hurt. And I began to understand: I would never be likable enough to have their love. Because I was a girl, and even a broken, bleeding girl needed to keep quiet.

It was the beast who came to the rescue the night I poured out the bottle of pills on my desk. It crept stealthily up the dark stairs into the light and nudged me with its cold nose. *Hey.* New teeth were coming in. They shone along its gum line like tiny seed pearls. "I have learned magic in the dark all these years," it said. I had not realized how much I'd missed its snarl.

"Write your pain," it said as it slipped into my pen. "Tell your story. Tell it with teeth."

"I'm afraid," I said. "I don't remember. I don't remember how to howl."

"Yes, you do," it promised. "I will remind you. But for fuck's sake, get angry. Don't die a martyr for their comfort."

The beast inside saved my life. Words saved me. Anger and truth saved me. The thing with teeth did not fear me. It did not abandon me when all else did.

Because I was a girl, they told me not to get angry. They told me no one would love me if I did. But I know who I am: I am the thing with teeth. I am the messy, too-much-feeling girl who can smile and growl at the same time. I am the dragon slipped free of its leash.

"Would you like to see what lives inside me?" I say, the beast scratching at the locks of my soul.

I part my red lips in a grin, exposing a mouthful of glorious teeth.

And then I throw open the basement door.

Maybe there is a thing with teeth coiled within you, too?

Don't be afraid.

Its bite may save your life.

I AM THE THING WITH TEETH. I AM THE MESSY, TOO-MUCH-FEELING GIRL WHO CAN SMILE AND GROWL AT THE SAME TIME. I AM THE DRAGON SLIPPED FREE OF ITS LEASH.

THE 1970s

- CONGRESS PASSES TITLE IX, A COMPREHENSIVE FEDERAL LAW THAT PROHIBITS DISCRIMINATION ON THE BASIS OF SEX IN ANY FEDERALLY FUNDED EDUCATION PROGRAM OR ACTIVITY.

- MORE WOMEN THAN MEN ENTER COLLEGE FOR THE FIRST TIME IN AMERICAN HISTORY.

- BILLIE JEAN KING FAMOUSLY DEFEATS BOBBY RIGGS, A VOCAL CRITIC OF WOMEN'S TENNIS, ON THE COURT DURING THE BATTLE OF THE SEXES IN HOUSTON, TEXAS.

- RENEE RICHARDS WINS A LANDMARK DECISION FOR TRANSGENDER RIGHTS WHEN THE NEW YORK SUPREME COURT RULES THAT SHE MUST BE ALLOWED TO COMPETE IN SPORTS TOURNAMENTS AS A WOMAN.

- THE EQUAL RIGHTS AMENDMENT, A PROPOSED AMENDMENT TO THE CONSTITUTION DESIGNED TO GUARANTEE EQUAL RIGHTS FOR WOMEN, IS DEFEATED.

- BARBARA WALTERS BECOMES THE FIRST WOMAN TO COANCHOR A NETWORK EVENING NEWS PROGRAM.

- NEW YORK CITY'S SHIRLEY CHISHOLM IS ELECTED AS THE FIRST AFRICAN-AMERICAN WOMAN TO CONGRESS, THE FIRST WOMAN TO RUN FOR THE DEMOCRATIC PARTY'S PRESIDENTIAL NOMINATION, AND THE FIRST AFRICAN-AMERICAN CANDIDATE FOR A MAJOR PARTY'S NOMINATION FOR PRESIDENT OF THE UNITED STATES.

- A SMALL GROUP OF WOMEN FORMS THE WOMEN'S LEGAL DEFENSE FUND, WHICH WINS A KEY COURT CASE ESTABLISHING THAT SEXUAL HARASSMENT IS ILLEGAL JOB DISCRIMINATION.

- RITA MORENO BECOMES THE FIRST HISPANIC WOMAN TO WIN AN EMMY, A GRAMMY, AN OSCAR, AND A TONY AWARD.

MELISSA DE LA CRUZ

Design-Options, the computer company that recruited me out of college, had an interesting hiring philosophy—bring in English majors and train them in computer programming. "It's easier to teach English majors programming than to teach computer majors how to communicate" was how Mr. Desmond, our beloved boss and patriarch, put it.

One of Mr. Desmond's other practices was to pay above and beyond the competition so that none of his employees ever left. We were loyal and grateful, and every year he took us to Le Cirque in New York City during the holiday season, where he would hand out fat bonus checks. During employee reviews, he would discuss art and opera, never clients or computers, and never once would he even mention anything about your performance other than to praise it. He and his executive team were old-fashioned gentlemen. It was almost like having lunch with your grandfather, if your grandfather was old and rich and lived in Boston. I have such fond memories of the man and the job.

Once my training was complete, I was sent off to Bankers Trust in New Jersey. At Bankers Trust, we were in charge of keeping the thirty-year-old finance programs running. We programmed in COBOL, one of the original computer languages, so old that our manuals dated from the 1960s. But the bank's servers still ran on it, and so they kept a staff of consultants to maintain it. The only actual bank employee on our team was the supervisor, a woman named Pat, who was unmarried and had a lot of cats. There were almost no married or working moms in our department, only young, single female programmers like me (there were three of us), Pat, and loads of men—married, old, young, single, the whole gamut.

I liked my job. The computer programmers I worked with were an eclectic bunch, from forty-year-old dads, who shared their kids' gymnastics pictures and regaled me with stories about tournament trips to Russia, to young Jersey guys, who wore gold chains and went out to the clubs five nights a week. I have pictures from this time of my life: the same group gathered for "Crazy Hat Day," "Crazy Sunglasses Day," and "Crazy Hawaiian Shirt Day."

Then Mr. Mercury joined our group (not his name, his name was Hermes—get it?—names have not been changed to shame the guilty, LOL). Another consultant, just like us, he had an attitude and a reputation for being brilliant but difficult, and from the moment he joined our team, he and I butted heads. He didn't like the casual camaraderie in the office. He spent hours on the phone on personal calls and then complained that none of us worked hard enough, especially me, since everyone knew I was writing a novel when my computer work was done for the day. (To be fair, most of us did something else—maintenance programming work was easy and rarely needed, and at any given time, Solitaire was open on almost all our computer screens.)

Pat, to her credit, asked me to stick it out. Once we put this project to bed, I would never have to work with Hermes again. But I made no pretense of my loathing for him and took to pointing out every mistake in his code, a game of

MELISSA DE LA CRUZ ■ *Because I Was a Girl*

gotcha that he played as well. I made sure to document every flaw in his design, and he made sure to tattle every time I was on the phone making plans with friends. I thought I could stomach it, and I gave as good as I got, but after a while, his daily complaints about my job performance—when I had had a stellar record until he arrived—got to me. Mr. Desmond learned I was having issues and begged me to stay as well, at least until the next bonus season, which was coming up in April.

But I had never encountered such loathing before—and believe me, Hermes *hated* me: because I had graduated from a better college, because I was younger, because I was smarter, and because I was a girl. His machismo could not understand how I could write better code than he and still find time to write my book, play Solitaire, and have a personal life.

It was a toxic environment, and the memory of the harassment I suffered still makes my breath catch a little and turns my stomach. I quit my job (giving up my April bonus) and found another small consulting firm to work for.

I was hired as a tester, which was a bit of a step down from a programmer. (The new company used software I was unfamiliar with.) As a tester, I worked with one of the database programmers, whom I'll call Ron (he looked like Will Ferrell's Ron Burgundy character). He was a white guy in his thirties, married, with babies, who lived in Jersey, and I was twenty-five and Asian and lived in Manhattan.

We had absolutely nothing in common but the work we did together. But we were friends. I found him hilarious, and he found me the same. There was no sexual tension between us at all. I can say this with utter conviction—our relationship was the very definition of platonic. We were good coworkers, and we cracked each other up. DAILY. Ron treated everyone the same, male or female, with his signature trash-talking, needling, and mocking.

Then, one day, it stopped. I popped by Ron's cubicle and started teasing him, as I did every day, expecting him to needle me back, before asking him to

HIS MACHISMO COULD NOT **UNDERSTAND** HOW I COULD WRITE **BETTER** CODE THAN HE AND STILL FIND TIME TO WRITE MY BOOK, PLAY SOLITAIRE, AND HAVE A PERSONAL LIFE.

reset the database. Instead of playing along, he said, very politely, and in a somewhat small voice, "Yes, I will restart the database."

I was like, "Dude, what is up with you?" But he wouldn't even look me in the eye.

I asked around, wondering if anyone knew what was up with Ron. I was so confused. Where had my friend gone?

Finally, I learned that someone had "spoken to him about his behavior." Apparently, some of my colleagues were uncomfortable with the nature of our friendship. One of the supervisors had told Ron that he had to stop treating me in such a casual manner, that it was inappropriate, that I might find it *harassment*.

WHUT?

I was so shocked. No one even asked me what I thought. I couldn't believe our joking around had gotten him in trouble. To this day, I am frustrated and sad that the corporate environment we were in did not know what to make of a friendship between two coworkers of the opposite sex.

A few years later, I left computer programming behind for good when I sold my first novel to Simon and Schuster. I'm happy to write that I've not run into any barriers in the publishing industry because of my gender. Though it has now been two decades since I switched to writing full time, I still receive emails from my former coworkers in the computer trenches. Frank from Jersey, with the gymnastics kids, sent me the sweetest congratulatory email when my first book was published. Jaime, who planned his wedding on his downtime (while I wrote my novel), did the same. Chris, a fellow recruit from Design-Options, sent the nicest note about how proud he was upon seeing my name on the bestseller list.

I never heard from Ron. He'd quit the firm a few months before I did. I never knew what happened to him, nor did I ever get a chance to talk to him about what had happened, because we never even had another conversation after he'd been dressed down. And that still makes me sad. To this day, I'm sorry we couldn't be friends at work because I was a girl.

ABBY FALIK

When I turned twelve, the parents in my Berkeley neighborhood started calling, inviting me to babysit their kids. I remember a conversation with my childhood friend Jacob. "It's so unfair," he said. "Why don't they ever call *me*?" But we both knew the answer: I got the gigs because I was a girl.

I was always excited about opportunities to work. My younger siblings and I were fortunate to have everything we needed, but purchases beyond the basics were up to us. Our allowance was equal to our age in dollars each month. So, when I was twelve, I got twelve dollars a month, or three dollars a week . . . which, I quickly discovered, was what I could make in a single hour babysitting.

I was thrilled when the phone started ringing. At the end of a Saturday night after feeding babies mashed peas or wrangling toddlers to bed, I was exhausted but lit up. I felt responsible, accountable, and accomplished—and it felt great.

Just before the end of seventh grade, I had an idea. What if, rather than babysitting for individual families, I had kids from multiple families come to me? Wouldn't that be more fun . . . and efficient? What if I hosted a day camp for neighborhood kids who needed somewhere to go once school was out for the summer? What if I hired my sister and friends and paid them to be counselors?

Instead of being paralyzed by these "what ifs," they became my road map. And rather than waiting for permission, I forged ahead. Within weeks my new "employees" and I had come up with a name for the camp, a schedule of activities, and a flyer that we had slipped into every mailbox in our neighborhood.

When summer started, Oakridge Kids Camp opened its doors to twenty young campers. We made *oobleck* out of cornstarch, and puppets out of old socks; we set up elaborate scavenger hunts and took field trips to the library and the fire station. We won rave reviews, and a year later, when we found ourselves with a waiting list for our second summer, we added more sessions and counselors. Within a few years, the camp had become a neighborhood institution. When I went to college, I passed the baton to my younger sister.

To be honest, I didn't think much of any of this at the time. It felt so natural to me—to see an opportunity and to find the people and resources to make something exist where it hadn't before. I didn't think about all the reasons we could have failed—and there were plenty—I just stayed focused on a clear vision of what was possible. And it worked.

Flash forward fifteen years, and I'm sitting in a classroom at Harvard Business School watching the professor write these words on the board: *Entrepreneurship: the pursuit of opportunity, independent of the resources under control.*

In that instant, something inside me clicked. These words described something I had felt from long before I had even heard the word *entrepreneur*.

I looked around at my classmates in Aldrich 007. As a girl, I was outnumbered two to one. And as someone who had never worked in a traditional for-profit business (I had opted instead for what I like to call the "for-purpose"

INSTEAD OF BEING PARALYZED BY THESE "WHAT IFS," THEY BECAME MY ROAD MAP. AND RATHER THAN WAITING FOR PERMISSION, I FORGED AHEAD.

DIDN'T THINK ABOUT ALL THE REASONS WE COULD HAVE FAILED—AND THERE WERE PLENTY— I JUST STAYED **FOCUSED** ON A CLEAR VISION OF WHAT WAS **POSSIBLE.** AND IT WORKED.

track, since I hate the term *nonprofit*), I should have felt like both an outsider and an underdog. But suddenly, I saw myself more clearly—as an innovator, a risk-taker, a builder—and my self-doubting gremlins vanished. I felt emboldened and confident that I was exactly where I was meant to be.

Today I'm the founder and leader of Global Citizen Year, the launchpad for bold high school graduates who are hungry to experience the world beyond our borders and use those experiences to shape their lives. Each year we select our country's most promising young leaders as Fellows and support them living and working in communities across Africa, Asia, and Latin America during a year before college. Immersed in a new community and contributing to local projects in fields like education, health, and the environment, our Fellows break down the barrier between "us" and "them," and between the classroom and the world. Ultimately, we envision a world where this global year becomes a hallmark of American education.

Building an organization from scratch has required more resourcefulness and grit than I could have ever imagined—but it has also been the most gratifying step of my entrepreneurial journey. I wake up every morning on fire to be doing work that never feels like work, and I go to sleep at night exhausted but fulfilled. I spend my days with talented teammates who push me to be my best and brightest self. And on the hard days—whether I'm facing a failure, frustration, or disappointment—I remind myself of Sheryl Sandberg's perfect question: "What would you do if you weren't afraid?" When I break through the fear, the next steps become clear.

Because I was a girl, I found my power in being soft and strong, caring and bold, grounded and visionary.

And once you find your power, no one can ever take it away.

REBECCA SOFFER

It was a beautiful October afternoon in 2004. Kids played in piles of crimson leaves, bodegas displayed pumpkins and bright yellow mums, and couples at outdoor cafés waded through the *New Yorker* over poppy seed bagels and schmear.

I was uptown, covering a murder.

The assignment was part of the core "Reporting and Writing" curriculum at the Columbia University Graduate School of Journalism. I'd dreamed of going there since the sixth grade, when I'd included it on my list of life goals (right underneath *Saturday Night Live* principal). We had no doctors, lawyers, or engineers in my family. What we did have were writers, editors, publishers, and a lot of opinions.

J-school immersion was no joke. While some of my friends enjoyed heavy doses of happy hours folded into their MBA programs, I was across campus, functionally overwhelmed by multiple weekly deadlines on little sleep; enduring no-holds-barred critique sessions in class; and relying on myself during the long, solitary reporting and writing hours to "work the problems," a favorite mantra courtesy of Mrs. Jackson, my eighth-grade algebra teacher.

Regardless, I was having a blast. After all, everybody's got a story, and I wanted to learn them all. I'd sat inside the Society of the Citizens of Pozzallo in Carroll Gardens with a slice of Monteleone's cheesecake on my lap, listening to septuagenarians with lifelong $100 monthly rents lament the neighborhood's shifting demographics. I'd attended a heated community board debate on local public schools during which a man became so upset while challenging an issue that he'd actually bolted out of the room crying. I'd strapped on a Marantz the size of my torso to produce a radio report on a "Dogs Against George W. Bush" rally in Central Park, a precursor of my first job after graduation, at *The Colbert Report*.

One assignment involved listening to police scanners and reporting on the first big crime mentioned. My beat was Washington Heights and Inwood, near the northernmost tip of Manhattan. And despite my hopes for a colorful bank robbery involving neither weapons nor victims but rather perpetrators à la Daniel Stern's and Joe Pesci's *Home Alone* characters, it was a murder. And murders really weren't my thing.

That afternoon I got off the subway at Dyckman Street, headed up the stairwell of a six-story walk-up, and knocked on the door of the victim's neighbor. My RW1 professor always pushed us to learn as many of the little details as possible while reporting on a piece. Since the victim had lived alone, I figured the neighbors might provide some insight into the kind of person he'd been and that it would be an emotional palate cleanser after reporting on the gritty and harrowing details of the crime.

Nobody answered, so I figured the residents were out. Then I heard a baby screaming from behind the door. At that same moment, a man rounded the top of the stairwell and headed toward me. "Hey, is this the Gonzalez[1] residence?" he said, offering me a business card proclaiming his status as a freelance reporter. "I'm here for the *New York Times*."

---

1   Name has been changed.

"I think so?" I uptalked, to my shock. What the hell? I suddenly felt self-conscious. I was twenty-eight at the time, and there was no way this guy was older than thirty. We were essentially peers. Suddenly, the flimsy, cream-colored "Rebecca Rosenberg, Reporter" J-school business card I offered in return felt like impostor identification next to his fancy, thick-stock one. He said nothing while glancing at it, but believe me when I tell you his expression clearly stated, *Oh, that's adorable.*

I tried to tell myself there was no reason for me to feel insecure or to pay attention to the tiny voice inside my head. The one reminding me I was five foot one and looked about twenty years old. The one suggesting my pink lip gloss disqualified me from looking the part of Serious Reporter. The one saying, "Stick to lifestyle features, little girl. Let the men handle this one."

"So you're reporting on this piece?" he said. "By yourself?"

And there it was. Just two words, but they spoke volumes.

"Um, yes. It's my crime assignment."

Cute, his smirk implied.

I was at a loss for what more to say so I knocked again. Realizing I was tasked with reporting alongside a guy who would likely try to push me aside to get his own story, I felt like running to the comfort of Pulitzer Hall back on campus. But what more could I do? My story was due by five, and deadline was king at J-school. *Work the problems.*

This time, the door opened. A twenty-something Hispanic woman stood there with bloodshot eyes, looking downright exhausted and holding a baby boy whose cries were clearly upsetting her.

"¿*Qué es lo que Uds. quieren*?" She was pissed by the interruption.

"Ma'am, I'm here to ask some questions about your neighbor, Victor García[2]," my new adversary said, physically edging me out of the doorframe. The baby kept shrieking.

I was stunned. This woman was in obvious distress with a colicky baby but this guy had the chutzpah to ask for a couple of quotes?

[2]   Name has been changed.

I poked my head into the doorway. "*Señorita, perdona la molestía. Veo que estás en un momento muy difícil. Te vamos a dejar en paz, a menos que te pueda ayudar en algo con el bebé,*" I assured her, preparing to get out of her hair immediately, though offering some help I assumed she'd reject. The man looked surprised. It was my turn to return the smirk. *That's right, buddy. I'm fluent in Spanish.*

The woman seemed rather relieved. "*Entra, entra.*" I went inside, and she closed the door on Mr. *New York Times. Hasta luego, amigo.*

A few seconds later, I found myself on the sofa with newly washed hands, trying to comfort the baby while his mother made herself a sorely needed *café con leche*—and one for me, too. She spoke about Victor as she drank it, and afterward as she folded some laundry while I kept holding the baby. She remembered how he'd borrow salt whenever he was making *carne guisada*, and how he loved overusing hair gel, and that he was hoping to get married in the next year. Miraculously, the baby finally drifted off to sleep in my arms, and we transferred him to a bassinet.

A half hour later, I headed out, armed with every detail I needed. "*Gracias,*" I said.

"*A ti,*" she said, and touched my hand. We smiled at each other.

As I walked back to the subway, I was reminded of something my dad used to say to me. He was an entrepreneur who founded a successful ad agency when he was in his twenties. Like me, he was baby-faced, and he pulled in an older-looking friend to land his first clients. My dad was also a feminist who ascribed to the Annie Oakley credo of "anything he can do, she can do better." During my various moments of self-doubt growing up, he'd quip "*Illegitimi non carborundum,*" which loosely translates to "Don't let the bastards grind you down." I used it as motivation whenever I had to aggressively push back at some barrier, often while listening to Led Zeppelin at high volume.

My final five-hundred-word article on the murder wasn't memorable. I don't have a file of it and, having written dozens of others that fall, can't recall most of its details. I'm also sure that intrepid freelance reporter got a great story

DURING MY VARIOUS MOMENTS OF SELF-DOUBT GROWING UP, HE'D QUIP *"ILLEGITIMI NON CARBORUNDUM,"* WHICH LOOSELY TRANSLATES TO "DON'T LET THE BASTARDS GRIND YOU DOWN."

THERE ARE A LOT OF WAYS TO
FIGHT BACK
TO AVOID BEING
GROUND DOWN.
AND SOMETIMES THE
SOFTEST ONES
ARE THE MOST
EFFECTIVE.

through other means. But when the woman touched my hand after we both helped each other out, I finally got it: There are a lot of ways to fight back to avoid being ground down. And sometimes the softest ones are the most effective.

I finished the class with highest honors.

ENTREPRENEUR
Photo credit: Annie Shak

TINA HAY

More and more, women are entering fields that were mainly or solely driven by men. Whether it's becoming a Supreme Court justice or annihilating the box office competition as a superhero, women are showing their strength in every field. Well, almost. There is one field where this is especially lacking: finance. It is still rare to meet a woman who is actively investing her money, trading stocks, or managing a portfolio. Whether young or old, rich or poor, most women are not making smart (or really any) investment decisions. Even in conversations with my highly educated friends, there are mostly blank faces when the stock market comes up. As women, we are happy to discuss the answer to "Who wore it best?" but are often absent from the "Who invested it best?" discussion.

I was just as uninvolved and uninterested in investing and managing my money as any of the women I encountered. Even the vocabulary was daunting . . . P&L, APY, CAGR? More like WTF? But what I would soon learn is that most people are clueless about money, but few are willing to admit it.

When I was growing up, my smartest financial decision was asking my parents to invest my bat mitzvah money in Coca-Cola and IBM stock. They didn't do it, and to this day I teasingly remind them about how much my investment would have grown by now if they had listened to me (a lot!). Otherwise, I was never proactively investing or managing my money. But everything changed when I found myself sitting in a finance class while getting my MBA at Harvard Business School.

I came from a liberal arts background and was struggling with the coursework, unlike the former bankers and consultants around me who were breezing through the material. I am a visual learner. I don't think in numbers, and I find financial concepts intimidating and overwhelming, especially as someone new to the jargon.

My way of learning was to use images and sketches to understand and solve problems. So I used scraps of paper, envelopes and napkins . . . anything I could get my hands on. I called it Napkin Finance. There were not many places or people I could turn to for help. And I was not alone. Many people struggle with numbers and basic financial concepts, but it is mostly women who have lower financial confidence and who pay the highest price. Interestingly, most women do recognize that they are less informed than men and are open to learning given the opportunity. This self-awareness and initiative is what is unique and, ultimately, empowering.

What started out as a passion project to empower myself has now become a platform and resource for both men and women. Napkin Finance is an easily accessible tool to help people understand basic financial skills, build their own knowledge base, and make better financial decisions. It has been especially exciting to discover that diverse groups of people are now using our platform. Women and men, both young and old, are coming to us for help in making important financial decisions.

Financial illiteracy can be very expensive. While it may start with a lack of general knowledge, a lack of confidence and access to skills ultimately means fewer women working in finance and bringing new perspectives. How many women work on Wall Street or are CEOs of the largest investment banks? How many financial advisors are women? How many hedge fund managers or private equity partners are women? How many venture capitalists are women? The low numbers are staggering. I notice this more now, working in finance and technology, as one of the few women in the room.

Resources, a network of mentors, and capital are more accessible to men, which means businesses headed by women have a harder time getting off the ground. And because there are fewer female investors and decision makers, fewer women-led businesses get funding. Time and again, the only thing that differentiates a successful business from a failure is having enough money to weather the storm and find the product market fit. Since most venture capital money goes to men, it is so much more difficult for women to take a company through the ups and downs that are typical of most start-ups.

My own struggles have been internal as much as external. I have had to overcome my fears and the voices that drown out my potential. I've had to block out the noise and find an inner strength—it's not easy, let me tell you. But I was incredibly lucky to grow up with parents who told me—and showed me—over and over that I could do anything I wanted. I believed them. They stood by me as a kid, when I was a bit of a tomboy and insisted that I play on the boys' team. They supported me when I decided one day to pack a bag and travel and live abroad. They cheered me on when I started a business and consoled me when that business bombed. I look back at all the crazy ideas I've had in my life, and my parents were always there for me. They are the reason I believe in myself, even when I have no reason to.

As mentioned above, a big challenge for women in business is a lack of confidence, not competence. Sitting around a table, women will be more humble and dismissive about what they have done. Men are encouraged to broadcast their

HAVE HAD TO OVERCOME
MY FEARS AND THE
VOICES THAT
DROWN OUT MY
POTENTIAL.
I'VE HAD TO BLOCK OUT
THE NOISE AND FIND AN
INNER STRENGTH—IT'S
NOT EASY,
LET ME TELL YOU.

accomplishments and are apt to consider themselves trailblazers. I try to take my cue from them and speak loudly and proudly.

I draw inspiration from the incredible women I see in other industries: best-selling authors, activists, lawyers, and doctors. I look to their achievements as evidence of what is possible for women. There is no reason that more women should not be running finance or technology businesses. I am optimistic that more and more women are going to be finding their way into technology and other nontraditional industries. In the meantime, I'm enjoying the shorter lines for the ladies' room!

ANJANETTE
JOHNSTON

I grew up in a small, rural town where the girls dressed in jeans and played as if they were boys. I had horses and rode a bike and learned to mow the lawn as well as clean the bathroom. My friends were the kids I went to public school with from kindergarten through graduation. Everyone was taught to work hard, period.

Throughout school, I went after what I wanted—recognition from my teachers, the highest test grade, the academic award. My teachers pushed me with difficult math problems and English essays and made sure I applied to top-level colleges. I understood that if you wanted to succeed, you had to go for it. And it worked—I graduated as valedictorian and was the first person from my family to attend college.

College was the same. My roommate and I were science majors, and we made our marks by participating in research projects and attending conferences. There was no question we would succeed, and the fact that we were women never crossed our minds. I graduated magna cum laude from Juniata College and went on to graduate school at the University of Virginia. Working toward my PhD, I was mentored by a community of diverse male and female scientists. The only time I was treated differently because I was a girl was by the male undergraduate students when I was a teacher's assistant. Their comments and behavior were easily brushed off. Currently, I work as a staff scientist at the National Institutes of Health (NIH).

So is this story, in which I was never treated differently because I was a girl, common? Or am I in the minority?

According to the Association for Women in Science, women make up 28 percent of scientific researchers worldwide. About half of biology graduate students are women, whereas only 18 percent of full professors nationwide are women. Compared with other STEM disciplines, salaries in biology are lower and competition for jobs is higher. Sexism is exemplified by statements from Nobel Laureate Tim Hunt, who noted that girls in the laboratory are an issue because "when you criticize them, they cry."

I've been lucky. Unlike what the statistics show, about half of the employees in my group at NIH are women, as is our immediate supervisor. We are educated women with families who manage work, school, sports, etc. Though gender inequality exists in many research institutes, it is not present where I work. As in my childhood, I am surrounded by people who challenge, respect, and inspire me.

Despite my accomplishments, I did have an experience where I felt I wasn't supposed to do something because I was a girl. And it didn't happen when I was growing up or going to school or at my job.

It happened last year.

My children attend a small private school where parent volunteers help with various activities. I agreed to coach one of the boys' basketball teams since my son was on the team and I had played in high school.

I prepared—I found my old basketball playbook, I looked up drills online,

I put together practice and game lineups. I walked into the first practice with my whistle and clipboard, ready for the challenge. Before practice, a father was looking for the coach, and rather than ask me (the adult with the whistle, clipboard, and basketballs), he asked another dad if he was coaching. I introduced myself, telling him how excited I was to be heading the team. He turned away dismissively and eagerly greeted the assistant coach, a dad who had arrived late and took over the drills I had started. For the rest of practice, I was essentially demoted to ball girl. I went home angry and questioning everything.

Did those dads assume I had no idea what I was doing?

Did I allow the prospect of being "head coach" to go to my head and show up unprepared?

Or was it simply because I was a girl?

I vented to my husband and to other moms and double-downed on my coaching responsibilities. Still, I felt the same disregard I had felt at that first practice from other male coaches during games, and I realized that it *was* because I was a girl that I was being treated this way. Gaining acceptance into the boys' club was going to require some work. That pissed me off, because I hadn't ever experienced this sort of blatant sexism before, not growing up, not at college, not while getting my PhD, and not ever at work. My instinct was to quit—I was supposed to be having fun, not proving I could coach nine- and ten-year-old boys.

But I didn't quit. I was patient and accommodating—sharing ideas for new skill work and splitting practices with the assistant coach. I willingly helped the less skilled players and let him focus on the more proficient players. Honestly, the boys did listen to him better and tended to goof off when I ran practice. That changed when we won some games; the boys even started calling me "coach" outside of practice. Not surprisingly, my son was my biggest supporter—he was the first to follow my instruction and not fool around during practice. Besides winning some games, having him back me up was my proudest moment.

It was 40-plus years before I was made to feel I was incapable of succeeding because I was a girl. It was lousy and made me feel incompetent. Looking back, I realize how ridiculous it was—especially since my reaction was to step back. I should have stepped up and used those years of empowerment to take control at that first practice and show that I belonged there with that whistle. I coached basketball again, and it was an overwhelmingly positive experience, primarily because of the support from the dads (who called me "coach" from day one).

Most important, my takeaway from this experience was that I showed those boys that a mom can do whatever she puts her mind to—graduate as valedictorian, be successful at her job, coach a boys' basketball team. She does it because she works hard and holds high expectations for herself as well as for them . . . even if they are boys.

MY TAKEAWAY
FROM THIS EXPERIENCE WAS THAT I SHOWED THOSE BOYS THAT A MOM CAN DO **WHATEVER** SHE PUTS HER MIND TO— GRADUATE AS VALEDICTORIAN, BE SUCCESSFUL AT HER JOB, COACH A BOYS' BASKETBALL TEAM.

CHILDREN'S BOOK EDITOR
Photo credit: Joyce Lee

ZAREEN JAFFERY

My parents made it clear throughout my childhood that the reason they emigrated from Pakistan to the United States was to give their children a good education. This was equally true for both my brothers and sisters—my parents didn't discriminate when it came to academic expectations. And lucky for them, all five of us were studious. Each week, my mother would take us to the local library, where we would check out as many books as we could carry—fiction or science or history, we had no restrictions. Every book was an opportunity to learn.

As I got older, my ambition turned into something sharper than that of my siblings. That drive stemmed from our family history. Particularly, my mother's history.

My mother was the first woman in her family to get a graduate degree. She attended university in Peshawar, Pakistan, in the 1970s and got a master of science in botany with the intention of having a career as a scientist. Since she regularly got the highest marks, she didn't think it would be difficult to find a job. But despite graduating at the top of her class and appearing in local newspapers in lists of students with academic honors, there was no job for her after graduation. She volunteered her time at a lab, taking a long bus ride each way, hoping that once the other scientists saw how great she was, they would hire her. That was not the case. They were happy to have her free labor.

Disheartened, she eventually quit the lab and decided to get married. She was soon introduced to my father, and once they were married, they moved to the United States, where she had five kids in eight years. Although she never got a job once she got to the United States (having five kids to take care of was plenty of work!), we grew up with beautiful rose and vegetable gardens in our yard, thanks to my botanist mom.

I had heard this story—of my mom's working for free in the lab—many times. My brilliant mother, who worked hard her whole life, was not able to get a job . . . because she was a girl. The unfairness of it stayed with me. Somewhere along the way, I became determined not only to get a great job after graduating college but also to succeed in whatever my chosen career turned out to be. I needed to do this as her daughter. To push back against societal standards that put people in narrow boxes based on gender or race or any other factor, and right what felt like a deep wrong.

I'm in my thirties now, the same age my mother was when she was telling my siblings and me stories about her childhood in Pakistan and taking us to the library to read as much as we could. My chosen career in children's book publishing is every bit as inspired by my mother as by my drive to succeed. And in 2016, after fourteen years of working in publishing, I launched a history-making children's book imprint, Salaam Reads, which publishes positive representations of Muslim kids and families, the first imprint to do so.

The news of the imprint was first introduced in the *New York Times*'s "Arts" section in February 2016, and from there, word spread. Given that the imprint's

MY BRILLIANT MOTHER, WHO WORKED HARD HER WHOLE LIFE, WAS NOT ABLE TO GET A JOB . . . BECAUSE SHE WAS A GIRL.

I HAD RARELY LET MYSELF CRY IN THE WORKPLACE. I HAD INTERNALIZED THE CRITICISM THAT BEING EMOTIONAL WAS GIRLISH AND UNPROFESSIONAL

launch comes at a time in US history when the rights of Muslims, and other marginalized communities, are under attack, book lovers around the globe received news of the imprint as a step toward empathy and compassion in a world that seemed hostile to differences. My work on Salaam Reads was also mentioned in *Dawn*, the oldest English-language newspaper in my mother's homeland of Pakistan. It turned out I had made the papers, too.

When I first announced the creation of the imprint at a meeting at my company, I couldn't hold back my feelings. I had rarely let myself cry in the workplace. I had internalized the criticism that being emotional was girlish and unprofessional. Although I tried to stop crying, it didn't work, and I cried through the entire presentation. Maybe I was emotional because I am a girl. Or maybe because I am my mother's girl, and I had succeeded.

THE 1980s

- IN 1980, FOR THE FIRST TIME, A HIGHER PERCENTAGE OF WOMEN THAN MEN VOTE IN A PRESIDENTIAL ELECTION—AND A HIGHER PERCENTAGE OF WOMEN THAN MEN WILL VOTE IN EVERY FUTURE PRESIDENTIAL ELECTION THROUGH 2016.

- THE NATIONAL WOMEN'S HISTORY PROJECT SUCCESSFULLY CAMPAIGNS FOR MARCH TO BE DECLARED NATIONAL WOMEN'S HISTORY MONTH ON THE FEDERAL CALENDAR.

- THE FIRST COED CLASS OF THE US MILITARY ACADEMY AT WEST POINT GRADUATES 62 WOMEN AS SECOND LIEUTENANTS IN THE US ARMY.

- AT 21 YEARS OLD, MAYA YING LIN WINS A PUBLIC DESIGN COMPETITION FOR THE VIETNAM VETERANS MEMORIAL AND FACES INTENSE DISCRIMINATION BECAUSE OF HER GENDER, LACK OF PROFESSIONAL EXPERIENCE, AND ETHNICITY.

- FLORENCE DELOREZ GRIFFITH JOYNER (FLO JO) SETS WORLD RECORDS FOR THE 100- AND 200-METER DASH AT THE 1988 OLYMPICS, RECORDS WHICH HAVE YET TO BE CHALLENGED.

- APPOINTED BY PRESIDENT RONALD REAGAN, SANDRA DAY O'CONNOR SERVES AS THE FIRST WOMAN JUSTICE OF THE US SUPREME COURT.

WRITER AND NATIONAL
POETRY SLAM CHAMPION
Photo credit: Stephanie "She" Ifendu

ELIZABETH ACEVEDO

The studio was dark and small, with just enough room for three chairs and a console full of buttons that added more bass or increased the volume. The producer sat in the one swivel chair, which allowed him to easily reach his laptop and control the recording. I sat in one of the other chairs, and one of my brothers in the third. Two other dudes stood behind the producer. I was fifteen and the only girl in the room, and they were all waiting for me to open my mouth.

When I was fifteen, I had my heart set on being a rapper. My brothers bought me instrumental mix tapes for my birthday, chaperoned me to open mics, and asked me to recite what I had scrawled in my notebook late at night using the light of my cell phone. I was committed to my dream of telling stories through music, and it was by no means a secret.

All the guys in my neighborhood knew me as my brothers' sister and as the "li'l rapper"—a title that was part condescension, part endearment, and mostly the way people in hip-hop are nicknamed. I was thrilled whenever a drug dealer on my block stopped me on my way home and asked me to "spit something." Elated when the older basketball players in the Little Park would bob their heads, grunt under their breaths, and clap me on the back with a "yooooooo!" whenever I spit a particularly dope verse. In a neighborhood where wannabe rap stars were as common as bird shit on fire escapes, I stood out, yes, because of my age . . . but mostly because of my gender.

I was the only girl I knew practicing her flow and internal rhyme, and not just listening to rap but *studying* it. Anytime I met another girl who spit, my initial reaction wasn't kumbaya sisterhood, it was an immediate sizing up of the other young woman to determine if she was a threat to my standing as The Girl Rapper. I was indirectly taught that there was not room for more than one. It seemed only one or, at most, two women dominated in hip-hop at a time, and to be the best, I had to crush all the other girls around me. And despite how much love my neighborhood showed me, being the only girl was a lonely position to hold and one that was quickly challenged when I reached high school and people started coming for my content, not just my style.

When I was fifteen, and finally ready to start recording music, it was in that little studio in Spanish Harlem that I was told for the first time, "You're good, but if you want to make it, you need to go harder. Spit some real shit." The silence that trailed the producer's words felt like it'd been plugged into the amplifier: It was loud and clear. By "harder," I was being told that the stories I focused on were too soft, too feminine, too much girl. I needed to be grittier and tougher and to pay homage to the tropes that made men in hip-hop—and many other musical art forms—famous: sex, drugs, and violence. The themes I commonly wrote about? Being catcalled, the injustices in my community, the abuelitas who sold pastelitos, and my immigrant background. Those stories were my most honest truth, and now I felt ashamed of them because I was being told they weren't enough.

Soon that same critique began to pour in from other producers and rappers

IN A NEIGHBORHOOD WHERE WANNABE RAP STARS WERE AS COMMON AS BIRD SHIT ON FIRE ESCAPES, I STOOD OUT, YES, BECAUSE OF MY AGE . . . BUT MOSTLY BECAUSE OF MY GENDER.

THOSE STORIES WERE MY MOST HONEST **TRUTH,** AND NOW I FELT **ASHAMED** OF THEM BECAUSE I WAS BEING TOLD THEY WEREN'T ENOUGH.

in my community. I was told I needed to talk about how my hands could silence other girls, and how my ass would make boys holler.

Rap was the house I walked into when I felt unheard in the world. It was the home where I pulled my dreams across the windows so I could sleep at night. It was hard to be evicted from my home because I didn't fit the singular idea most people involved in rap had of A Girl Rapper. So I quit. Perhaps if I'd been older and more in charge of how my sexuality could be deployed, or if I had been braver and defiant in the face of the guys who shook their heads no, or if I'd had a stronger sense of ownership in the craft, I would have been able to push past the lack of representation and the feeling that there was no place for me in this music I loved. But I was fifteen, without any immediate role model in the game to mentor me, and with only men determining how far I could go. To this day, I wonder, *What if I'd kept going?*

I continued telling my stories—I just shifted how they were told. When I moved to spoken word and poetry, I was able to transfer my love of rhyme there. I rode that love to a bachelor's degree in performing arts and a master's degree in creative writing. I now perform poetry at high schools and colleges and community centers and teen prisons, and when I tell students that I found poetry through my love for hip-hop, without fail, a student, often a girl, raises her hand and asks me if I still rap. Usually in my show I'll recite an old verse or two, so it's not a surprising question, but I always feel a jump in my chest, like the *tick tick tick* of the metronome. I shake my head.

"No, I don't rap anymore," I say with a shrug. "But maybe it's not too late."

STAND-UP COMEDIAN, WRITER,
PERFORMER, AND PRODUCER
Photo credit: Sharon Attia

JENA FRIEDMAN

A few months into working at *The Daily Show*, I was struggling. It was the most exhilarating and challenging place I had ever worked, but my background as a writer and performer had not exactly prepared me for the job I had been hired to do. The "field producer" role required a set of skills beyond writing and performing. It also included directing, producing, and editing, as well as shooting in strange and sometimes hostile locales, coaxing performances out of nonactors who were often either camera shy or just reluctant to play along, working with unfamiliar local crews of varying skill levels, and dealing with a slew of other variables. Oh, and the work we created all had to make sense *and* be funny. I found it really hard at first; not only did I have no experience in the technical elements of filmmaking, but I was also the only female producer in my department and often the only woman, besides maybe the correspondent, on the majority of field shoots.

In one early segment, we were filming in a cancer clinic (I know, LOLZ) to illustrate a point about how the potential government sequester cuts would hurt cancer funding (those were simpler times). I was so out of my element and in my head during shooting that I forgot to get a crucial shot for the story. After botching the piece, I wondered if I was cut out for the job at all. It turned out my bosses shared similar concerns and called me into their office the next day to talk about it. They told me that they believed in me (I was lucky to have such great bosses) but that I had to "be more aggressive in the field." With those notes, they sent me back out into the world to produce my next segment, which I knew would make or break my career at The Daily Show.

The story was about North Carolina's dubious new restrictive voting laws. The joke of the piece was to expose these laws not as racist, as most critics were calling them, but rather as "Democratist," or intended to hurt all Democrats (it was a term we coined). Our comedic solution was to level the playing field (off of a John Lewis sound bite that we conveniently misinterpreted) by making it more difficult for Republicans to vote as well. For one of the jokes to work (in which we call on Democrats to limit Republican votes by moving voting booths to Planned Parenthoods), we needed an establishing shot of a Planned Parenthood, under which the correspondent (let's call him Aasif) would post a sign that read "Vote Here." Our schedule was tight—we had been running around all day looking for locations, and we had to get them all before our flight that evening. So we were overjoyed when we learned there was a Planned Parenthood nearby in Asheville.

As we rolled up to the clinic, I saw a few pairs of eyes poking out of the blinds. I ran inside to assure the staff we weren't doing anything shady. I walked up to the receptionist and repeated my standard script: "Hi, we're with The Daily Show. Is it cool if we film an establishing shot—"

"We know who you are," she said before I could even finish my sentence. "We're fans. We just want you to know that someone just threw a bag on our steps, and the bomb squad is on their way to make sure it's not explosive."

My heart stopped. I froze, unsure what to do. Then I remembered my boss's directive: "be more aggressive." I raced outside and assessed the situation. It didn't look like a bomb (I later learned it was actually a bag full of shit, literally), Aasif was already in position, and the shot would take only a second to grab.

"Roll tape!" I calmly instructed the DP at the top of my lungs. We shot one take, and then I told everyone to quickly run to the van, and we got the heck out of there. As we drove away, the bomb squad rolled up, and the crew suddenly understood why I hadn't insisted on multiple takes. Thankfully, no one was even remotely upset that I might have put their lives or limbs in danger. (Okay, Aasif was a little annoyed.)

When I looked over the footage in the van, I saw that we had gotten the shot!

The piece turned out great. It actually ended up going viral, and my bosses were thrilled. A year later, a judge even cited our segment in a court ruling to overturn the state's unconstitutional voter ID laws.

That segment was a turning point for my career at the show. I worked at *The Daily Show* for two more years and produced a lot of great segments. I learned to be more assertive out of the gate when making first impressions with a new crew. I also discovered that I could use being female to my advantage. A lot of people I encountered in the field (more often than not, men) seemed to find women less threatening than men. As a result, I was able to gain access to people and places my male colleagues might not have been able to. I'm not sure how that makes me feel—I can be all kinds of threatening—but I was sure happy to get the shots and interviews. Never again would I put my crew in danger for the sake of a joke, but the experience did teach me to have confidence in my skills and instincts as a producer . . . and to always remember to donate to Planned Parenthood.

EMILY CALANDRELLI

I was an afterthought.

When I walked into a room of professional scientists and engineers, they addressed my male field producer first. They introduced themselves to my cameraman first. They showed off their fancy spacecraft to our audio guy before including me in the conversation. I was the host of the show—the girl in four pounds of makeup and three-inch heels. But I was an afterthought, sometimes ignored entirely. They didn't realize that I was the only one in the group who had spent years learning about ion propulsion, lunar-lander technology, and different ways to design a rover's wheel to make it survive harsh Martian conditions.

It wasn't until I started asking about their technology with questions only a person who had studied nearly a decade in the field would be able to ask that they paid attention to me. Even then, I was once asked if the male engineers in the room fed me my technical questions. I would think, *If I were a tall, burly man, would you have made that same assumption?*

I was told that it was my own fault that I was ignored. I wasn't "assertive enough" when I entered a room; I needed to "be more confident."

The worst feeling would come on shoots when men would say, "Well, you certainly don't *look* like an engineer!" Meant as a compliment, I would instead hear, "You pay attention to hair, makeup, and girly things. You couldn't possibly have the brain capacity or interest to focus on science, too."

I'm not saying these sorts of things were intentional. I believe they are the result of subconscious bias or, hey, maybe even social awkwardness! Perhaps the men were merely intimidated by my fabulous fake eyelashes. Experiences like these didn't happen on every shoot. In fact, it didn't happen *most* of the time. It *never* happened with my female experts, and I'd met a few male self-proclaimed feminists, who treated me as an equal. But every time one of these things did happen, it was a hurdle to overcome for the day, and something that would stay with me long after the shoot.

Then something funny happened. These sexist interactions started happening less and less. I suspect it was because the show started to do well. It got picked up season after season, and it won a few national awards for science education along the way. Instead of crafting pitches to persuade companies to film with us, businesses were reaching out to *me* requesting to be included in the next season. We'd created a science show with a solid reputation, and people were paying attention.

Our show's reputation, and my reputation as the host, preceded us. My interview subjects would kindly ask about my time at MIT, my TEDx talk on space exploration, and my thoughts on searching for life beyond Earth. I was no longer an afterthought. I was seen as an individual with a genuine interest and basic understanding of science and space, someone whose voice mattered.

The experts began to look me in the eyes and include me in the conversation. They described their technology to me and stopped doubting the origin of my questions. All this happened . . . and I didn't even have to change the way I entered the room. I walked, talked, and introduced myself just as I had done before.

THEY DIDN'T REALIZE THAT I WAS THE **ONLY ONE** IN THE GROUP WHO HAD SPENT **YEARS LEARNING** ABOUT ION PROPULSION, LUNAR-LANDER TECHNOLOGY, AND DIFFERENT WAYS TO DESIGN **A ROVER'S WHEEL** TO MAKE IT SURVIVE HARSH **MARTIAN CONDITIONS**

PERHAPS THE MEN WERE MERELY INTIMIDATED BY MY FABULOUS **FAKE** EYELASHES.

Today women often have to work just a little bit harder to get included in the conversation, to sit at the table, or to be afforded the same credibility as their male peers.

When it comes to STEM, the bias can be even stronger. People seem to believe that women must be one-dimensional in their interests and surprised when girls can love coding *and* Kylie Jenner's new lip kit. We can fight cancer in the lab *and* get our nails done in the salon. And, of course, we can have a deep appreciation for fake lashes while understanding the significance of rocket reusability for the space industry.

JANE HAWLEY

The sweltering heat of our apartment puts us on edge.

I'm six years old, sitting at the counter. My mother, wearing a white cotton nightgown, is standing in the kitchen, cracking ice cubes out of a plastic tray.

I'm looking up at her, trying to tell her something, but she stares at me blankly.

"Mom," I say. "Are you listening?"

Her eyes glaze over. Her center of gravity tips.

She falls onto the yellow linoleum, dropping the tray and knocking a glass off the counter. The glass shatters. Ice cubes skitter across the floor.

Her body convulses, shaking, shaking, shaking.

I call an ambulance, which transports her to the emergency room, where the doctor reports her epilepsy to the DMV. They immediately revoke her license.

She never drives a car again.

My mother would die two years later from complications related to lupus. In the time between her first grand mal seizure and her death, I watched her lose much of her independence. My mother had a big personality—she wore silk blouses and full makeup nearly every day and possessed a fierce sense of justice. Her illness not only prevented her from doing many things she loved—mainly working as a head paralegal at a top law firm—but the epilepsy also prevented her from traveling anywhere not on the city bus route. She had to rely on others to take us to the grocery store, to the doctor's office, to the movie theater. Though Mom found ways to get around some of the limitations, I watched her struggle with living life on her own terms. Her illness was closing in on her, preventing her from living expansively. Her life, she felt, was shrinking.

I also felt confined. Because I couldn't go anywhere myself, I used books to push against the limits of my life—and I found myself leaning on them even more after my mother's death to navigate my grief. Yet something was missing in the books that were either assigned at school or recommended to me. Adventure seemed only to belong to men. Sal Paradise. Huck Finn. Raoul Duke. Men were having adventures, leading messy lives, getting into trouble, and finding them-selves on the open road. Not girls.

I hungered for a road narrative that was representative of me, for a book that might lay out a map for my own life. When I was sixteen, a girlfriend from my high school creative-writing class recommended Joan Didion's *Play It As It Lays*. I read the novel in one sitting, exhilarated by the passages of Maria Wyeth, the novel's heroine, driving alone, endlessly circling through the infinite circuits of Los Angeles highways: the 405, the 101, I-5. She uses the time both to process her life and to get her mind off her ghosts. It's not what I would call an uplifting novel. Maria isn't a particularly good person. The ending isn't redemptive.

That's not Didion's point. Not even close.

It's that you have to live life on your own terms. You have to be in control of the cards. No one else can play your hand. You have to play the game for yourself.

Once I got my own driver's license and the keys to a used Volkswagen, I was almost never home. Dad trusted me not to get into too much trouble. I pushed the limits of where I could drive and back in one day, with only a few maps crumpled under the passenger seat to use for navigation, sometimes going as far as my home in Bakersfield to Los Angeles and back before curfew.

It only made sense to go away for college when I graduated high school. Dad wanted me to enroll at the local community college, to stay at home. I wanted to skip town. I wanted to get away from anything that was familiar, anything that was safe.

When I was seventeen, I moved to Wyoming for college. After graduation, I returned to California for a few years, then packed up my car and drove myself to Texas for graduate school. My family and friends expressed their concerns. Was I aware of what could happen to me? There were so many things to fear on the open road: breaking down, blowing out a tire, losing or crashing the car, getting lost, getting assaulted. Since childhood, I had been conditioned to feel that going out by myself for any extended period of time was a threat simply due to my gender.

So I stopped asking for permission or approval. I just drove.

In my twenty-eight years, I've moved across the country four times and have taken countless road trips on my own. I've driven alone across the Mojave Desert at sunrise and seen the technicolor lights of Las Vegas at night, curving around Utah's red rock hoodoos, speeding through the High Plains at eighty miles an hour, watching thunderheads race across the big blue sky. I've driven across West Texas at night, cutting across vast landscapes of nothing and everything, a blanket of stars twinkling overhead. I've struggled through Reno during a snowstorm and stopped in Marana, Arizona, where the asphalt melted the bottom of my shoes.

I've baptized myself with the great holy dirt of America.

My family's fears? Most of them happened at one time or another. I've broken down, run out of money, run out of gas, been stopped at the border, gotten

MEN WERE HAVING
ADVENTURES,
LEADING MESSY LIVES,
GETTING INTO
TROUBLE,
AND FINDING
THEMSELVES
ON THE OPEN ROAD.
NOT GIRLS,

speeding tickets, and gotten lost. But I also found my way and found myself. I've had to face myself, listen to my thoughts, and figure out what I'm driving away from and what I'm driving toward. I stopped looking at these obstacles as something to fear. Instead, I simply began to see the fear as a challenge to overcome, as an essential part of not only my life on the road but also my life's journey.

As a young woman, I was taught to fear the world around me. We teach our girls not to take risks to keep them safe. Traveling alone as a woman is dangerous. It's also radical.

The ability to travel and to idle, to wonder and to wander, is necessary to lead an independent life. In *A Room of Her Own*, Virginia Woolf famously argues that every woman should have a little money and space for herself: "I hope that you will possess yourselves of money enough to travel and to idle, to contemplate the future or the past of the world, to dream over books and loiter at street corners and let the line of thought dip deep into the stream."

I say every woman should have a car (or bike or bus pass or MetroCard) of her own.

JODY HOUSER

'm one of the lucky ones. The first time someone said to me "I didn't
know girls liked comics," I was well into adulthood and could laugh off
his comment as incredibly naive. At that point, I'd been reading comics
for over a decade, had spent the past three years running a comic shop's
online store, and had recently completed my thesis for my MFA, an original superhero screenplay. So to me, this comment was an outlier, a joke
to toss out in conversation later on.

Other women I know weren't quite as lucky. Their first experience in
a comic shop was with a retailer who wanted to exclude new fans rather
than embrace new readers. Or choosing to express their opinions about
comics or other areas of pop culture made them a target for harassment.
Or someone thought their cosplay at a convention was an invitation to
be touched or mocked or tested to see if they actually knew the character.
There are far too many stories like this. Stories that show me just how

lucky I've been to feel consistently welcomed both as a professional and as a fan.

It was women fighting for their place in the comics industry that gave me my first big break. I'd been dabbling in comics for a while, creating webcomics and pitching my first anthology. A friend shared a tweet by a female comic artist who was looking to put together an anthology for charity with other female comic creators. Though I didn't have a lot of experience yet, I thought I'd throw my hat in the ring. I sent the artist, Renae De Liz, an e-mail saying I'd love to participate. I was one of over a hundred women who did so that first day.

That anthology became known as *Womanthology*, which in 2011 set the record for funding of a comic-book project on Kickstarter. The campaign hit its funding goal in nineteen hours and ended up receiving over $100,000 in pledges, more than four times the initial goal. Big comic and pop-culture names, such as Jim Lee and Kevin Smith, contributed pledge incentives and promoted the Kickstarter. What was initially going to be a small press collection became a massive, 400-page hardcover put out by mainstream publisher IDW.

Again, I was lucky. I tried my hand at comics right as people were asking where the industry's female writers and artists were. I signed on to a project that hit the zeitgeist in just the right way, attracting press and readers that no one expected. One of the artists I worked with on the book, Fiona Staples, blew up right after we collaborated thanks to her work on Image Comics's *Saga*, the first issue of which came out the same day as *Womanthology*.

But the thing about luck is that so much of it can reach us because of the women who worked hard to pave the way before us. We're lucky to have people like Trina Robbins, who worked to preserve the history of women in comics. Women have been a part of the industry since the Golden Age of comics, which saw the birth of the superheroes that today grace our movie screens. Girls have been reading comics since the beginning. (Of course, everyone read comics back in the day.) If the road seems smooth, it's because of the work put in by those who came before us. And because we're lucky enough to avoid the potholes that are still scattered about.

There's still a lot of work to do. Comics is a niche industry these days, and new, diverse voices are the only way to ensure it stays relevant. Much as we see in other areas of media, books written by and/or catered toward women are still seen as "other" or "lesser." Or that dreaded word *pandering*.

But women are louder and more visible in comics than they've ever been. A female retailer group, the Valkyries, is influencing what stores carry and thus what readers purchase. A female creator group, Comic Book Women, allows women to network with others in the industry and helps conventions find guests and panelists. Where once a small handful of female creators were familiar names, I'm now part of a crowd.

I'm lucky to be here, forging a career in an industry where the occasional person may not think I belong. Girls really like comics, both consuming and creating them. And I hope to make the path even smoother for the next girls who come along to tell their stories.

LAWYER

LORETTA MIRANDA

When the economy of the Morongo Indian Reservation in California grew large enough to provide full-tuition college scholarships for descendants, I did what any reservation kid who is told she is "gifted" does: I went to college for the sole purpose of moving to a more exciting area. College was my chance to get out, to escape, to finally make it on my own. I wasn't going to squander it.

During college, my mentor (a woman) and American Indian Student Association advisor was the first person to urge me to go to law school so I could give back to my own community. At the time, however, I had no interest in American Indian law. In fact, I never even had the desire to take an American Indian Studies course, though my university offered a minor in the field. I'm not entirely sure why I had no interest. I set aside her suggestion.

But time moves fast in college, and graduation came quickly—I graduated having no clue what I wanted to do. I found a few retail positions to support myself, but then I discovered a nonprofit drug- and alcohol-treatment center that was run primarily by Natives. As someone who has had friends and family members lose the battle to drug and alcohol addiction on my own reservation, I decided to contact the nonprofit about available positions.

I somehow got a job as an outreach coordinator. I finally had a job that I enjoyed and that I was naturally *good* at, working with other Natives; my personal experience helped. I excelled in my position and was often asked to take on additional duties because my supervisor knew I could handle a larger workload, including the most difficult tasks: homeless outreach, weekly presentations to recently paroled individuals and inmates at the county jail, and training new intake coordinators. I never said no to any task. But after two years, I eventually realized that no matter how many additional responsibilities I took on, the promises of raises and promotions were empty. This was particularly frustrating because I witnessed a number of male coworkers get promotions, along with constant praise, even though, IMHO, they did not do their jobs well. On top of that, management often viewed suggestions and new ideas from the women on staff as personal attacks. Like most women, I have been treated differently in various situations because of my gender. But this was the first time my gender was a hindrance to my professional success. And the fact that I experienced it while working with my community, the Native community, was disappointing because Native women often hold our community together.

Still, working at the nonprofit helped me see my purpose in life: to give back to my own community, to make it better, stronger. Realizing that I would likely never see a promotion at the nonprofit, I contemplated my next move. Another mentor (also a woman) helped me see that I could give so much back through the law, echoing my college advisor. And I wanted to be in a position of power, in a place where no one could overlook me ever again because of my gender. So, three years after graduating from college, I took the LSAT. Unfortunately, my brother passed away weeks before the exam and I didn't score as high as I knew I could. I took the exam once more, refusing to give up or settle for a low score. The thing about loss is that sometimes you can find inner strength from

THIS WAS THE FIRST TIME
MY GENDER WAS
A HINDRANCE TO
MY PROFESSIONAL SUCCESS.
AND THE FACT THAT I
EXPERIENCED IT WHILE
WORKING WITH MY COMMUNITY,
THE NATIVE COMMUNITY, WAS
DISAPPOINTING BECAUSE
NATIVE WOMEN
OFTEN HOLD OUR COMMUNITY
TOGETHER.

I'VE LEARNED TO CHANNEL THOSE STRUGGLES INTO POWER.

it. Paired with the resentment born from the experiences I had at the nonprofit treatment center, I had the strength I needed to persevere. Needless to say, I did well on the exam and decided to attend Lewis & Clark Law School because of its prestigious Indian law program.

Being an (almost) attorney, I can say without doubt that working women face many struggles daily. In my budding law career, my struggles might not be as blatant as the ones I faced while working at the nonprofit, but they exist nonetheless: Worrying about whether you're smiling too much, if your voice is too high, or whether the neckline of your blouse is too low. But I've learned to channel those struggles into power.

I graduated from law school in May 2016 and am working at an amazing Indian law firm in the Bay Area as a law fellow. I am fortunate to be working in the same field that brought me to law school.

My next hurdle is the California Bar exam. It's knocked me down a couple of times, but I am persistent and will not give up until I've conquered that beast. I went to law school to give back to my community, and I will overcome this one last obstacle in order to give back as much as I can. I'm honored to serve my community and grateful that I can use my education to help others. And although there are times when being a girl creates certain obstacles for us, it also creates opportunities to better ourselves and surpass the arbitrary limits we've set.

LENORE ZION

The school psychologist sat quietly across from me, the cow's eyeball on the desk between us. It wasn't the first time I had been sent to her office. There was the time when I had caused my teacher a significant amount of discomfort by describing in vivid detail my future death, which I had predicted would result from a particularly bloody and horrific act of aggression. The time before that, I had enthusiastically led a group of my classmates in a game I'd invented wherein we were all imaginary chain saw–wielding maniacs hell-bent on carving one another into pieces. When I brought the cow's eyeball into school, my teacher didn't even ask where I'd gotten it before she sent me to the psychologist. Had she asked, I probably would have denied the truth: that I'd stolen it from a classroom in the local community college, the halls of which I was roaming because my parents had enrolled me in a Saturday morning art class in the same facility. After all, I was no idiot; stealing was a punishable offense.

It was sitting on a shelf in a science lab. A jar of murky preservative liquid with this odd fleshy beige thing floating inside. At the time, I didn't know it was an eyeball—there was nothing about its appearance that I could immediately identify as eyeball-esque. But I knew it was a biological something-or-other, clearly a piece of something once alive. There were about twenty, twenty-five of them, all lined up in a row. I was only seven, but I knew I could get away with taking one. Honestly, I didn't feel a moment of guilt—I just swiped one of the jars, stuffed it into my backpack, and that was that.

When my father picked me up at the end of my art class, I pulled the jar out.

"What is this?" I asked him.

My dad took a look.

"That's an eyeball," he said.

My father just so happened to be a retinal surgeon. If he knew anything, he knew eyeballs.

"From a person?" I asked, a sense of morbid excitement swelling.

"Sweetheart, no. Look how big it is. You think that would fit in your eye socket?" he said.

I laughed.

"Maybe a cow, or a sheep," he said. "There aren't many sheep in town, so probably a cow."

"Still pretty cool," I said.

"It's very cool," he said. "Where did you get it?"

"They gave it to me," I lied.

My father didn't seem to think anything about that was suspicious. "We can dissect it later if you want," he offered.

I was so proud of my cow's eyeball in a jar. I was very excited to dissect it with my father, but I wanted to show it off a bit before I took it apart. This was a real treasure; my dad thought it was cool, I thought it was cool, my mother and my sister and my brothers thought it was cool. Not for one second did I consider that my teacher wouldn't respond similarly when I shoved the jar in front of her

WHEN MY FATHER PICKED
ME UP AT THE END OF
MY ART CLASS,
I PULLED THE JAR OUT.
"WHAT IS THIS?"
I ASKED HIM.
MY DAD TOOK A LOOK.
"THAT'S AN EYEBALL,"
HE SAID.

I BECAME CONVINCED THAT
THE AUTHORITY I WAS
BUTTING UP AGAINST
MUST HAVE GLEANED THAT I'D
STOLEN
MY TREASURE.
THIEVERY WAS MY
ONLY CRIME.

face, liquid sloshing all around. Instead, her face contorted into an expression of horror.

"It's not a human eyeball. It's just a cow's eyeball. Or a sheep's, but probably a cow's eyeball."

She didn't respond to my explanation. Due to my previous visits to the school psychologist, during which I learned that little girls who fantasize about death and violence were odd, I assumed my teacher was displeased because she was under the impression that I'd come to be in possession of this eyeball through violent means.

"No, no," I assured her. "Someone else gouged it out, not me. Actually, someone cut out a whole bunch of cows' eyeballs. There's a whole lot more where this came from."

And then I was in the psychologist's office with my eyeball. After several attempts at explaining my superexciting plans to carve up the eyeball with my father later, I stopped trying. Instead, I sat in defeated silence, waiting for my mother to come pick me up. I was in big trouble; there had to be a reason for that. I became convinced that the authority I was butting up against must have gleaned that I'd stolen my treasure. Thievery was my only crime. When my mother arrived, the psychologist told her that in all her years of practice, she'd never had a student sent to her for terrorizing her teacher with a preserved eyeball. My mother laughed.

"This is not a joke," she told my mother, and continued to explain that it was very unusual for seven-year-old girls to be so thoroughly invested in gruesome fantasy.

"See, now, I wouldn't call it that," my mother said.

"What would you call it?"

"Biology," she said.

And with that, we left. Me and my awesome mom. And my eyeball in a jar, soon to be dissected during a fun and educational afternoon with my awesome dad.

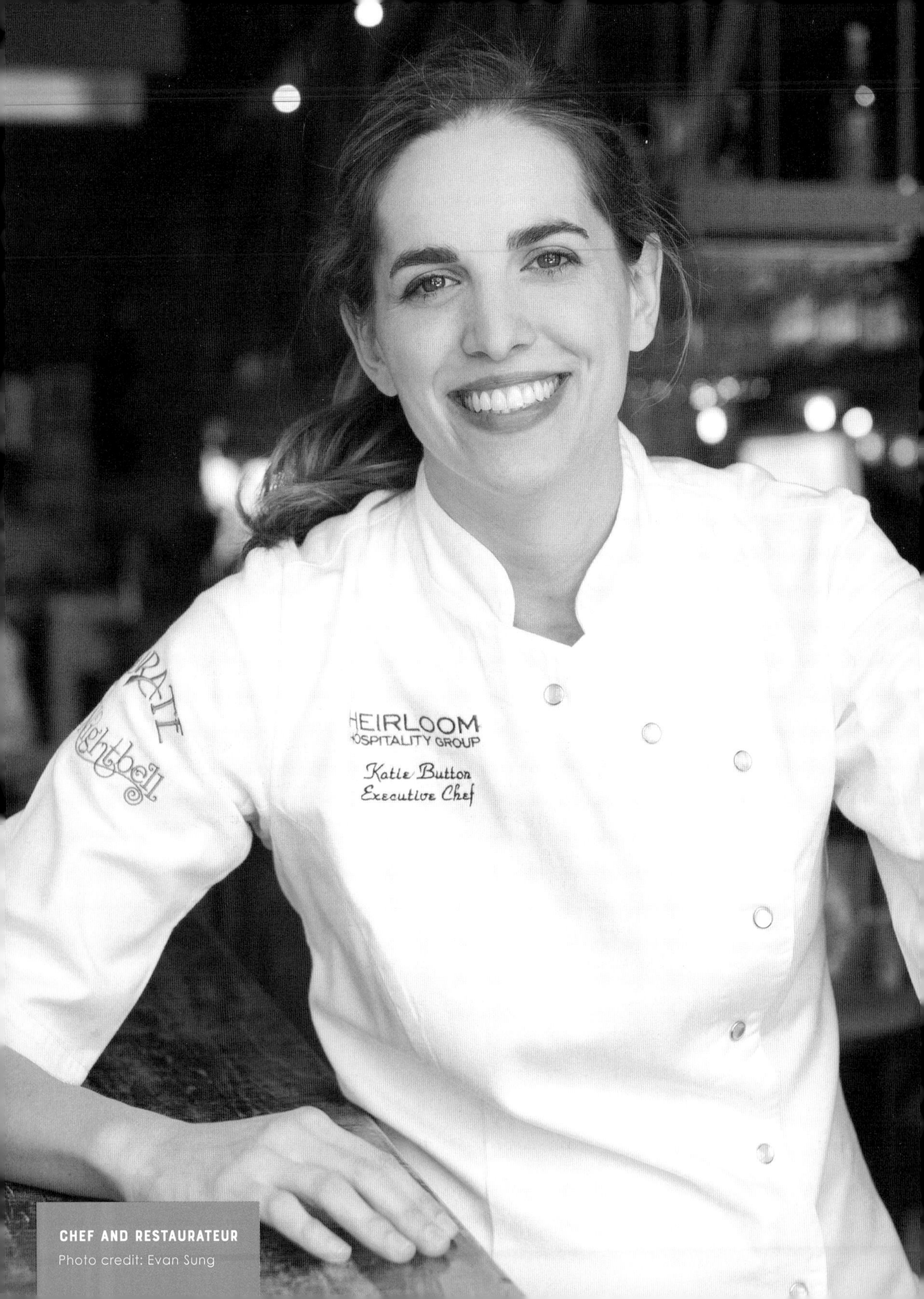

CHEF AND RESTAURATEUR
Photo credit: Evan Sung

KATIE BUTTON

There have been many moments in my life when I have been faced with a question: Do I take the path that is expected of me? Or do I try to find my own way, following my strengths and passion?

For years, I did the former. When I was twelve years old, I really wanted to be a cheerleader. Some of my friends were trying out for the basketball cheerleading squad. While I had little interest in basketball, cheerleading sounded like fun and also like the type of activity I was supposed to do.

I raced home that day to talk it over with my parents. They had the annoying habit of questioning my choices, of trying to make me see all sides of a decision. I was nervous about the conversation because I was so determined to join the cheerleading squad with the other girls, and I didn't want them to ruin that.

As we sat down to dinner, I presented my case. Actually, I begged my parents to let me try out. If I didn't join the cheerleading squad, I told them, I would be excluded from *all* my friends' social activities for the rest of my life, and it would be their fault for raising an antisocial outsider as a daughter.

My folks considered my plight for about thirty seconds. I saw their blank stares turn to pity and then to resolve when they firmly said "no way." They knew my strengths—and deep down, so did I—and suggested that I would be better suited to hustling on the lacrosse field than attempting to do splits. At first, I felt crushed. But then I thought about it, and as usual, I had to admit that my parents were right. I joined the girls' lacrosse team and loved it.

I went on to attend Cornell University to pursue a degree in chemical engineering. I figured, hey, I'm pretty good at math and science, and I hear that engineers get jobs when they graduate. At the time, I thought I was leaning on the lessons I had gleaned from my adolescence, namely, to make a choice that suited my individual strengths. As a girl, I had considered cheerleading because I thought that was what girls were meant to do, and it was what my friends were doing. And now, here I was, pursuing an engineering degree, something girls didn't often do. But I hadn't thought through my plan. I had no idea what an engineer did for a living and hadn't even considered if I would enjoy being one.

As graduation approached, I had no sense of what I wanted to do with the degree. My classes hadn't inspired me, and my job interviews were going terribly. So I sat down with a professor whom I admired and asked him the big question: "What should I do with my life?" I remember throwing it at him like I was trying to make casual conversation, just a nonchalant chat about the rest of my life. Meanwhile, the backs of my knees were sweating, and I had ripped a piece of my notebook paper into five hundred teeny tiny pieces.

He gave me a meaningful look and said, "You should go into pharmaceutical sales."

My heart sank. An image flashed across my brain of me in a professional yet embarrassingly flirty outfit convincing a group of doctors that my drug brand is better because it only kills people less-than-sometimes whereas the competitors' brand kills people more-than-sometimes. That was definitely *not* what I wanted

THERE HAVE BEEN MANY MOMENTS IN MY LIFE WHEN I HAVE BEEN FACED WITH A QUESTION: DO I TAKE THE PATH THAT IS EXPECTED OF ME? OR DO I TRY TO FIND MY OWN WAY, FOLLOWING MY STRENGTHS AND PASSION?

to do, and I had this nagging suspicion that he made the suggestion because I was a woman.

I didn't take his advice, and I was nowhere closer to getting a job. So I did what many people in that position do: I kept studying. It's the moment in life that I call "When in doubt, get a master's degree." I got mine in biomedical engineering. When I still wasn't sure what I wanted to do after that, I applied and was accepted into a PhD program in neuroscience.

As the start date of the program loomed, I found myself feeling more and more stressed out. I wasn't taking care of myself; I wasn't sleeping or eating. I finally decided to take a step back and think about my life.

Just before this moment, I had taken a monthlong trip to Zambia to build houses for Habitat for Humanity. While I was there, I was surprised to see families and children who were happy despite the fact that they appeared to have little in the way of material possessions. When I looked back on that trip, it dawned on me that I was profoundly unhappy in my career path. Here I was, someone who had been given every opportunity in life and could choose to do whatever she wanted to do but couldn't seem to find happiness. I realized that if I started that PhD program, I was going to spend seven years (or more!) pursuing something I wasn't passionate about, followed by a life in a job that I wouldn't enjoy. I knew I could not fake happy for all my life. So, without knowing what I was going to do, I quit the PhD program two weeks before it was supposed to start.

For the first time in years, my life had no structure. Even though I hadn't particularly liked my studies, they had given me a sense of purpose. My parents praised my good grades. It felt good to brag to friends about my accomplishments. It was amazing to say the words "PhD in neuroscience" out loud and just watch the faces light up. But at the end of the day, I felt unfulfilled—I needed to find a path that brought me inner joy, not just gratification from others.

When I thought about every time I had been happy in life, I realized food was involved. Helping my mother with her catering business when I was growing up, trying out different recipes to keep sane while cramming for exams—those were the happy memories that had stuck with me. I decided to try to find a job in the restaurant industry. I set out, résumé in hand, to the best restaurants in Washington, DC. No one would hire me to cook, but the general manager at one of José Andrés's restaurants, Café Atlántico/Minibar, offered me a job as a server.

From my first day, I knew working in restaurants was what I wanted and needed to do for the rest of my life. I loved the energy, speed, pressure, and precision that went into the restaurant business; I only had to figure out how to make my way into the kitchen. Still, it felt as if the moment I made the career change—to go after something I really loved—doors started opening for me. I met Felix Meana, who is now my husband, who supported my career change and helped me meet the right people to make it happen. I moved into the kitchen during an internship at Jean Georges in New York City and then in Los Angeles at the Bazaar by José Andrés. I had the opportunity to work in the kitchen at elBulli, a Michelin three-star restaurant in Spain and the top-ranked restaurant in the world for five years. I took all this experience and moved to Asheville, North Carolina, to open my own restaurant with my husband and my parents.

Six years later, at the time of this writing, I am the chef and co-owner of two restaurants in Asheville. I was named one of *Food & Wine* magazine's Best New Chefs, I was a finalist for the James Beard Rising Star Chef of the Year, and I have published my first cookbook. Life is rolling right along, and I can't wait to see where this career takes me.

When I look back on that moment when I decided to drop out of my PhD program, I think, "Thank goodness I finally figured out what makes me happy and where my strengths lie." Doing so changed my life forever.

Bottom line: Do what you love, not what you think is expected of you. Follow your true passion no matter where it leads. It will help you find your strength in life and success, but more important, happiness will follow.

THE 1990s

- WOMEN REACH THE PEAK OF THEIR LABOR FORCE PARTICIPATION AT 60 PERCENT.

- 1992 SEES MORE WOMEN THAN EVER BEFORE ELECTED TO POLITICAL OFFICE FOR A TOTAL OF 47 HOUSE REPRESENTATIVES AND 7 SENATORS.

- RIOT GRRRL AND ZINE CULTURE QUICKLY SPREAD AS MUSICAL AND ARTISTIC MOVEMENTS TO END HOMOPHOBIA, RACISM, SEXISM, AND VIOLENCE AGAINST WOMEN AND GIRLS.

- IN 1997, SARAH MCLACHLAN CREATES LILITH FAIR, WHICH BECOMES THE TOP GROSSING OF ANY TOURING FESTIVAL THAT YEAR.

- CARLY FIORINA BECOMES THE FIRST FEMALE CEO OF A FORTUNE 50 COMPANY.

- GLORIA STEINEM AND MARIE WILSON OF THE MS. FOUNDATION FOR WOMEN FOUND "TAKE OUR DAUGHTERS TO WORK DAY" TO EXPAND THE CAREER HORIZONS OF GIRLS ACROSS THE UNITED STATES.

- THE WOMEN'S NATIONAL BASKETBALL ASSOCIATION (WNBA) DEBUTS WITH EIGHT TEAMS THAT PLAY IN THE SAME ARENA AS THEIR NBA COUNTERPARTS.

- THE US DEPARTMENT OF LABOR ESTABLISHES THE GLASS CEILING COMMISSION TO ELIMINATE BARRIERS THAT BLOCK QUALIFIED WOMEN FROM WORKPLACE ADVANCEMENT.

- THE NATIONAL INSTITUTES OF HEALTH ESTABLISHES THE OFFICE OF RESEARCH ON WOMEN'S HEALTH TO INCREASE WOMEN'S REPRESENTATION IN ALL MEDICAL RESEARCH.

VICTORIA AVEYARD

Because I was a girl, a millennial girl, the kind with a working mom and a supportive dad, with an education, with a dream, with a path, with people willing to pick me up and push me back when I needed it—I am who I am today.

Because I was a *lucky* girl, with white skin, a stable home, with almost a century separating my life from women's suffrage.

Because college was never a question.

Because homework was never an option.

Because my parents showed up to every game.

Because most of my problems were normal problems. A math test, acne, the school dance, college acceptance or denial.

Because the world I grew up in was almost entirely built for me, to shelter me, hold me, grow me.

Because there was a boy who got that scholarship over me, even though my grades were better.

Because people used to tell me, you better marry rich.

Because people used to say talking that much is unladylike.

Because teachers would ignore my hand when I was the only one who knew the answer.

And this shouldn't sting as much as it does, but because I had to watch men save the day in almost every one of my favorite stories. Because Princess Leia and Hermione Granger were the only ones I had to cling to, but at the very least, they looked like me.

I'm blessed not to have any stories about being denied a job or a college education, or about anything stolen on the grandest scale. I work in one industry that is female-driven. I work in one that is absolutely not, though steps are being made. And I live, unfortunately, in a time when it feels like steps are being taken backward. It could be that I'm simply becoming an adult, opening my eyes fully. It could be that I've been blind for a very long time, hemmed in by my own privilege. I'm sure that's the case with many things. But one thing is very clear, and made even clearer by the rise of social media: Women with voices, women with opinions, women who speak on any scale on any subject, are expendable. They are either branded as targets or marked as unimportant. They are either abused or dismissed or both, in far greater measure than any man of privilege. Both are meant to harm, and both are weapons used to silence.

I've learned this firsthand because I have social media of my own . . . and a tendency to shout. I've had my fair share of trolls, most of them hiding behind false names and false pictures and just plain falsehoods. They see women as easy pickings, particularly women of color, as well as groups far more marginalized than I. I've never faced abuse of that magnitude, nor can I imagine it. But this isn't just a hallmark of strangers on the Internet, whether they originate in an American basement or a Russian office building.

Because I was a girl, I've had a man I know tell me to stop talking about politics. To get a hobby, to go to the gym, to pick up *crocheting*. At first glance, it seemed

WOMEN WITH VOICES,
WOMEN WITH OPINIONS, WOMEN
WHO SPEAK ON ANY SCALE ON
ANY SUBJECT, ARE
EXPENDABLE.
THEY ARE EITHER BRANDED AS
TARGETS OR MARKED
AS UNIMPORTANT.
THEY ARE EITHER ABUSED OR DISMISSED
OR BOTH, IN FAR GREATER MEASURE THAN
ANY MAN OF PRIVILEGE.
BOTH ARE MEANT TO HARM,
AND BOTH ARE WEAPONS USED TO
SILENCE.

BECAUSE I AM A CERTAIN TYPE OF GIRL, MANY DOORS ARE OPEN TO ME. BUT BECAUSE I AM A GIRL, I KNOW THERE ARE MANY MORE STILL FIRMLY SHUT.

harmless. Another person unwilling to face facts or even properly debate a point was trying to brush me aside. But because I was a girl, because I've seen worse, because I'm a writer who understands intent and connotation, I reluctantly realized there was much more at play. And since I'm a loudmouth, not to mention a modern woman living now, I decided to point out his blatant sexism. I didn't really expect an apology. But I didn't expect to be laughed at, either. Or dismissed and ridiculed, name-called into oblivion. Essentially told that I, a working woman, didn't even know what sexism was. That *I* was the sexist for interpreting his comment in such a way. And I really didn't expect this person to call my father afterward, in some strange throwback to caveman patriarchy wherein men can only communicate from one chief to another. Because, apparently, that isn't sexism, either.

In the scheme of the world, this is a small instance and an insignificant one. This person holds no power in my life. But it revealed a hard-learned truth. Sexism is in the eye of the beholder. Because I am a girl, I know what it looks like. And I know that many people have no idea they are part of it, feeding it, and spreading it with every insidious, ignorant breath. They can't acknowledge what they don't see or refuse to understand.

I still mourn the loss so many of us felt on Election Day 2016, when we saw how much sexism weighs. When the smart, determined girl in class lost to the loudmouthed bully. When the little girls we used to be were cast aside by horrendous reality. I live with the pain of it every day, but worst of all is the pain I can't fathom. The little girls who exist right now, in every classroom, in every home, studying, creating, playing, dreaming. I hope the world did not dim for them as it dimmed for me. I hope they never hit a wall they can't climb.

Because I am a certain type of girl, many doors are open to me. But because I am a girl, I know there are many more still firmly shut. For one more day, or forever? Only the girls of the future will know.

JOAN HANAWI

A few years ago I was working under a grant to launch a digital literacy program in Pano, Ecuador. I was familiar with the community, having lived there two years prior, but as I was meeting a family new to the program, I wasn't even halfway through my introduction when they interrupted me.

"But where's Juan?" the Kichwa family asked, looking to my local partner, Edmundo, as the authority.

In South America, my name, *Joan*, is often misread as *Juan*. This mistake leads to confusion when the person who arrives does not fit the image of whom they were expecting, especially when that person is me, a girl.

This was nothing new to me.

At a very young age, I was told I should be a leader. On any given day, I was—and still am—buzzing with ideas, and it didn't take long for me to realize that the most effective way to bring these schemes to life was to learn how to channel resources and direct others toward a shared goal. In other words, to lead.

My training officially started in fifth grade. My teacher had to step out of the room, but before she did, she asked me, "Can you please look after the class while I'm gone?" My heart swelled with pomposity at the realization that I was being given this responsibility, and I eagerly nodded in agreement. As she left, my teacher announced, "Class, I need to run a quick errand, so in the meantime, Joan is in charge."

This may sound like a minor moment, but for me, it marks the root of my journey in leadership. Being put in charge of my peers filled me with pride and power—two traits I quickly learned should be at the bottom of any leader's priorities.

I regularly misunderstood the duties associated with many of my early leadership positions. I wanted to be someone important, which I thought meant you had to be domineering and controlling. It took me a while to figure out that real leaders are service-oriented and empathetic. While I had built a résumé that boasted student council presidencies and club leadership positions, nothing compared with the experiences I had abroad through my gap year.

I moved to the Amazon rain forest as a Global Citizen Year Fellow after I graduated from high school. The opportunity allowed me to work with the German International Development Cooperation and the Ecuadorian Ministry of the Environment. By taking the time to learn the culture of the people whom I was living with, I laid the relational foundations to return in the future and be trusted as a partner.

It was on one of these return trips that I found myself trying to explain yet again that I was actually the project lead, the so-called Juan. Ecuador is a nation where *machismo*, or masculine pride, runs strong. While it's important to be aware of the cultural context in which you're working, it's also important to recognize societal norms that allow women to be overlooked as leaders and to subvert that reality.

Because Edmundo respects me (the feeling is mutual), he would always inform the perplexed community members that I was, in fact, the director. With a gentle smile, I would explain that I was the girl they were looking for.

The students and their families were deeply curious as to how I managed to be in charge. When asked about how I came to my role, I shared my mother's story, explaining how she fought the odds to become a doctor and leader in not one but two countries. My ambition was modeled after hers. I had started with smaller positions to develop my skills and had worked my way up. I had earned the trust to take on larger, international responsibilities.

On the same trip, one of my local girlfriends, Rocío, commented, "You're such a young girl, but you're a leader. I wish I could be like you. It's because you foreign girls are raised differently. I could never do what you do."

To this day, that's one of the phrases that sticks with me—*I could never do what you do*—not because of its truth but because of its falsehood.

Because I was a girl, it's true that I was socialized to adhere to certain gender norms. Despite my global travels, I was told to be cautious for safety's sake. Despite my boldness, I was taught to temper my words for agreeability. Despite my merits, I was encouraged to take my appearance into account. But I think it's exactly these qualities that girls are often criticized for—sensitivity, emotionality, among others—that prime us to be good leaders.

To me, leadership is the ultimate form of service. It's the duty to speak for those who have no voice. And sometimes as leaders, we're privileged to see people grow into their voices. Despite her belief that she couldn't do what I do, Rocío became a leader. She's now the program coordinator of the project Edmundo and I built.

The critical piece of this story, however, is that I was empowered by my community to step into each of these positions. I didn't get here on my own; I'm here because of the tireless efforts of others before me. I've thrived because of the girls who supported me instead of threatening me, because of the boys who backed me instead of belittling me.

These days, I take my leadership lessons from the jungle, and I'm learning

"YOU'RE SUCH A YOUNG GIRL, BUT YOU'RE A **LEADER.** I WISH I COULD BE LIKE YOU."

what it means to be a leader in the workforce. I'm in my early twenties, and I've lived and worked on five continents. I've gone from pioneering new technology with indigenous communities to launching groundbreaking programs at global universities. Since finishing my degree, I've entered the corporate world to figure out how to leverage some of the most influential brands—and their resources—for good.

Whether viewed as a Juan or a Joan, I was told I should be a leader. So maybe I'll go from leading community projects to taking over as the CEO of a Fortune 500 company, or perhaps I'll become the world's best mom, or maybe I'll be America's first female president. But maybe it'll be you instead. Because you're a girl, too.

NOOR TAGOURI

Growing up, it had been my dream to work in television. Still, even as a child, I recognized that no one on TV looked like me or my mom or the other women in my family. I realized that people on television had to look a certain way, and if I was ever going to make it on TV, I could never embrace the hijab.

When I was fifteen, my family moved from a predominantly white neighborhood in Maryland to a city just outside DC. I experienced my own sense of culture shock, and I was exposed to a wide array of diversity. I was no longer the only dark-haired girl in town who spoke Arabic with Muslim parents who didn't celebrate Christmas. The move—the change—triggered something in me. I felt less afraid to feel or be different. And so I decided to wear the hijab. I still knew that wearing the hijab could complicate the prospects of my dream to be on TV, that it might tempt people to draw certain conclusions about me. But it was a struggle that I was willing to endure.

I started college when I was sixteen. That first year was amazing. I was learning a lot, and my fellow students, thankfully, never really treated me differently. As I started my sophomore year, I landed an internship at CBS radio. I remember going to Tennessee for a class assignment to cover a hearing about a mosque cemetery. The sense of security I had developed was dashed when a former GOP congressional candidate at the hearing refused to speak with me because, as she said, "I don't want to be on Al Jazeera." Another person at the hearing denounced Islam to my face, asserting that my religion was "no religion at all."

These kinds of Islamophobic comments became all too common as my career progressed. Often, people focused on the hijab, which meant I had to work harder to get the story. My team at work told me these kinds of issues never happened with the other reporters. They didn't have to spell out why.

In 2015, a young black man named Freddie Gray was violently arrested by the police and died a week later from injuries he sustained during the scuffle. His death triggered protests throughout Baltimore, which left the city in a state of emergency. The media coverage seemed unfair to me. Many protesters were described as "rioters," "looters," and "thugs," rather than what I saw them as: activists. As such, it was a story that definitely caught my interest, and I was determined to cover it.

On April 30, 2015, just outside City Hall, surrounded by various media outlets, the Reverend Al Sharpton spoke about the crisis in Baltimore. I decided to focus my coverage on a separate, passionate demonstration not far away, primarily made up of young black men and women who asserted that the reverend did not speak for them. They felt ignored by the media, which were more interested in covering the voices of celebrities and politicians. I could empathize to some degree.

I walked into the Baltimore protests with my videographer, determined to prove to myself and others that just because I was a woman in a hijab did not mean I couldn't get the story. We'd managed to get a few interviews at the demonstration, but I was looking for something *more*. Just then, two young onlookers beckoned us over. Hesitantly, we approached them. One of them pointed at what appeared to be a quiet road. "Walk down that street," he said with a smile, "and you'll find the most beautiful thing you've ever seen in your life."

Curious, we took his advice and soon heard the sound of a crowd. At the end of the street was another group of demonstrators, dancing and singing. As soon as we arrived, the crowd rushed over, clearly eager to set the record straight, to explain that the demonstrators were not rioters and looters but concerned citizens who cared about their community and were proud of their city. They just wanted to be *heard*.

Emotions washed over me. Here, my hijab was not a deterrent; it kind of felt like the opposite. I felt seen in a way I hadn't been before in my career. Maybe my hijab garnered trust from these demonstrators because we both understood what it meant to be misrepresented by the media. Maybe they trusted me because I was unafraid to present myself as I really was. Or maybe they trusted me because I was just as eager to listen.

In that moment, I realized that embracing my identity was not the disadvantage to my career I always feared it would be—I had just been thinking about it the wrong way. I had been trying to fit into a certain model, one that had formed in my childhood. But my experience in Baltimore revealed a new path. My hijab could be a beacon for others like me to relate to. My own differences could make me a better journalist.

After we collected our stories and interviews, my videographer and I hopped into our car and cried with relief and bliss. We'd done it. It was there, in Baltimore, that we'd finally found the stories we were meant to tell. Since then, I've focused most of my stories on those of the marginalized and silenced. I graduated college. I did a TED Talk. I did a keynote speech for the South by Southwest Conference. I've traveled globally to share my story and inspire others, and I have worked on a clothing-line collaboration to combat sex trafficking. And now I'm a reporter on Newsy, a leading online video news site, and the host of a Newsy original series: *A Woman's Job*.

And I'm thriving.

I started figure skating when I was about 5.

Unlike most of the girls I knew, I didn't start skating because of the sparkling Olympic women I saw on TV.

I got on the ice to follow in the footsteps of my older brother Joe.

Two years my senior, Joe was a figure-skating star. He had the knack that so many kids didn't.

What made my start as a figure skater so bizarre was that I didn't actually have any interest in ice skating. I wasn't inspired by the speed, the moves, or the glory. I liked ice skating about as much as I liked breakfast. It was fine. It was just there.

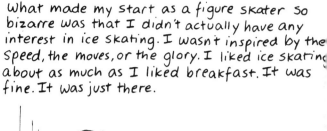

What drew me to the ice was something else entirely. I had been going to my brother's practices for some time to watch him skate. And watching him had hit a nerve somewhere deep and unknown inside me.

I thought for a long time that Joe was the inspiration, but it turned out to be a lot simpler than that. It was the way he looked. Short hair, black clothes, and matching black skates. That was what fueled me. I didn't want to jump or spin or compete. I just wanted to look like him.

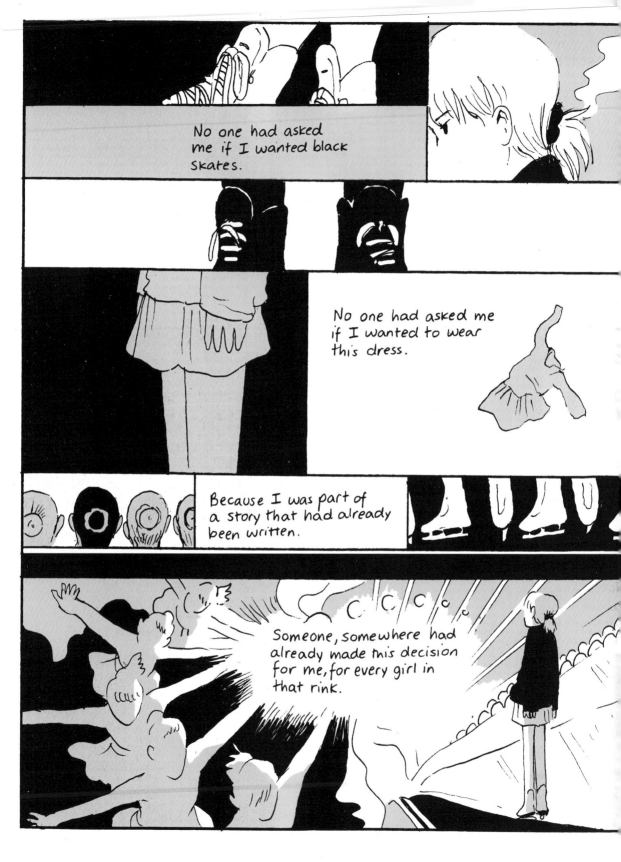

This could seem like a small moment, a small defeat. But so often the moments that define us aren't big and bright and blasting. They are, instead, small and brief and horribly sharp.

What hurts the most was how quick I was to accept it. That the color black didn't belong to me.

I couldn't even muster the courage to throw a tantrum.

I didn't even know how to tie my shoes yet. How could I fight history?

Ice skating taught me, with brutal clarity, that being a "proper" girl was about not being at all. Being meant questioning, desiring, leading. But the lights and winds of the rink, of the world, seemed to say that what I needed to do, instead, was simply follow the path that had been made for me, for all of us.

I would go on to wear those dresses and those white skates for 12 more years.

My brother would quit skating soon after I started, unable to cope with the pressure and stereotypes of being a male figure skater.

I never did get to wear black ice skates.

But after I quit skating, I did manage to buy black clothes and cut all my hair off as I always wanted to.

THE 2000s

- PRESIDENT OBAMA ESTABLISHES THE WHITE HOUSE COUNCIL ON WOMEN AND GIRLS TO ADVISE THE EXECUTIVE DEPARTMENT AND AGENCIES ON ISSUES RELATING TO THE WELFARE OF WOMEN AND GIRLS.

- THE MATTHEW SHEPARD AND JAMES BYRD JR. HATE CRIMES PREVENTION ACT EXPANDS THE DEFINITION OF A FEDERAL HATE CRIME TO INCLUDE VIOLENT CRIMES BASED ON GENDER OR GENDER IDENTITY.

- DANICA PATRICK BECOMES THE FIRST WOMAN TO EVER LEAD THE INDIANAPOLIS 500 AND EVENTUALLY WINS THIRD PLACE, THE HIGHEST ANY FEMALE DRIVER HAS EVER FINISHED IN THE WORLD'S BIGGEST RACE.

- NANCY PELOSI BECOMES THE FIRST FEMALE SPEAKER OF THE HOUSE OF REPRESENTATIVES, SONIA SOTOMAYOR IS CONFIRMED AS A SUPREME COURT JUSTICE, CONDOLEEZZA RICE SERVES AS THE FIRST FEMALE AFRICAN-AMERICAN SECRETARY OF STATE, AND ANN DUNWOODY BECOMES THE FIRST FEMALE FOUR-STAR GENERAL IN THE US MILITARY.

- AFTER A 56-YEAR-LONG ROMANCE, DEL MARTIN AND PHYLLIS LYON WED EACH OTHER AS THE FIRST SAME-SEX COUPLE TO BE LEGALLY MARRIED IN THE UNITED STATES.

- THE LILLY LEDBETTER FAIR PAY ACT, THE FIRST BILL SIGNED INTO LAW BY PRESIDENT OBAMA, RESTORES FEDERAL PROTECTION AGAINST PAY DISCRIMINATION BASED ON GENDER.

QUVENZHANÉ WALLIS

No one has ever told me I couldn't do something because I was a girl. I never really thought about sexism until I was older and learned that women get paid less than men for the same job, which is terrible. It's never happened to me, and I hope it never does. A lot of women from the past have fought and fought to make it possible for girls like me to do whatever we want. I go to an all-girls school, so the viewpoint and attitude that boys are better than girls don't exist at my school. I would say we're told the exact opposite. We're taught girls can do anything!

My parents also never said stuff like "Don't throw like a girl" to me. They always say, "Just do your best, and whatever happens, happens."

I want girls to know that it doesn't matter that you are a girl or how old you are. If it is something you like and dream of doing, just go for it, just do it! Your age, your gender—they don't matter. I wanted to be an

I WANT GIRLS TO KNOW THAT IT DOESN'T MATTER THAT YOU **ARE A GIRL** OR HOW OLD YOU ARE. IF IT IS SOMETHING YOU LIKE **AND DREAM OF** DOING, JUST GO FOR IT, **JUST DO IT!** YOUR AGE, YOUR GENDER— THEY DON'T MATTER.

actress since I was little, and I went after my dream. For my first movie role, I was nominated for an Academy Award. Since then, I've worked for a lot of great directors and starred alongside amazing actors. Years ago, I told my parents that I like writing and wanted to write books and scripts; now I have four books coming out. And I'm not done dreaming yet—when I grow up, I'd also like to be a veterinarian or a doctor.

STUDENT AND TRANSGENDER ACTIVIST
Photo credit: Ron Murray / ImageActive.com

ZOEY LUNA

High school has been much harder than I expected.

I entered high school wide-eyed and excited. I was feeling really good about myself at the time. After years of struggling to love myself, I had finally started being *me* and understanding who I was. I had navigated my transition in fifth grade. I had made all sorts of great friends, many of whom are still my friends today. They were going to the same high school I was, so it was basically middle school 2.0, but with new people. And I was looking forward to making even more new friends and getting a boyfriend. I was ready.

But I wasn't prepared for all the people who had it out for me because I am transgender. Immediately, I became known as "the trans girl." I didn't understand why I could only be the trans girl and not just Zoey. I know I'm transgender, but why does that have to be my only label? I started to blame myself, thinking that I was doing something wrong if people could see me only as transgender. What about all the other things that make me *me*?

Finding a boyfriend was proving really tough, too. I had been talking to some boys, and every time they would say things like "Let's keep things private" or "Let's be low-key." And I'd ask why, but I knew why.

One guy actually had the "kindness" to tell me point blank (via text): "Since you're transgender I don't want to be seen with you in public. Let's just chill at your place? Btw you're so pretty!"

I grew to hate myself again, as I did before I transitioned. No guys wanted to be seen with me in public because I'm transgender, my art wasn't taken seriously because I was transgender, I wasn't taken seriously as a human because I was transgender.

I made an effort to just fade away, which, if you know me, does NOT suit my personality. I explored myself through others. I made friends with about every clique in the school. The artsy kids, entitled upperclassmen, potheads, basketball girls, the Goth kids. I adjusted my personality to fit in with them—I just wanted to belong to something. But I found myself feeling even more lonely and lost. (I even cut my fringe just because I wanted to be known for something other than being transgender. The bangs were cute, but they didn't have the desired long-term effect.)

Time passed; I can't even tell you how much, because when you feel the heaviness of being lonely pushing you down, you lose track of, well, everything. But one day, something just clicked: Why do I have to let other people define me? Why do I have to feel sad just because others don't get me? I couldn't make a spot for *myself* in a group if I wasn't being *myself*. It was as if I had snapped out of a horrible dream. Suddenly, it all seemed so obvious. I finally understood that being transgender isn't a bad thing just because of what some generic boys or superficial kids thought. If people are going to associate me as only being transgender, so be it, because I know I'm much more than that. Being transgender is just a part of who I am. I'm also an actor and an artist. I'm warm and pretty. I'm a good friend and daughter. I care about people.

BUT ONE DAY, SOMETHING JUST CLICKED: WHY DO I HAVE TO LET OTHER PEOPLE DEFINE ME? WHY DO I HAVE TO FEEL SAD JUST BECAUSE OTHERS DON'T GET ME?

I'M MAKING IT MY **MISSION** TO STOP LABELING PEOPLE BASED ON WHAT'S ON THE **OUTSIDE,** TO STOP ASSUMING THINGS ABOUT THEM BECAUSE OF HOW THEY LOOK OR TALK.

It sucks to be put in a box by society, be it for your gender expression, color, ethnicity, style, voice, hair, decisions, or literally anything. I'm guilty of doing it, too. But I'm making it my mission to stop labeling people based on what's on the outside, to stop assuming things about them because of how they look or talk. We all have many different layers.

I have a few years left of high school, and yet I've already wised up so much. I'm confident in ways that I've never been before—back and better than ever. And the best part is, if I can shake off the weight of a thousand underhanded comments about my identity, I know I can handle anything.

MATTIE JOHNSTON

As told to Melissa de la Cruz

I told my mom I couldn't participate in this book because no one has ever told me I couldn't do anything because I was a girl. That's just silly!

When we saw *Hamilton* in New York, I told my mom that it should have been called "Eliza," because if it weren't for her, we wouldn't know Alexander Hamilton's story—she was the real hero of the play.

I really like *Stranger Things* because Eleven, the girl, is the most powerful. Every year for Comic-Con in San Diego, I dress up as an evil girl supervillain. I'd be happy to dress up as a superhero, but there aren't enough girl superheroes with cool costumes. I've gone as Harley Quinn and Poison Ivy. This year, I might go as Laura and Dad is going as Logan, aka Wolverine and his daughter.

The other week, the boys banned me from their clan on Clash Royale because I was a better player than they were, but I demanded that they reinstate me, and they did.

EVERY YEAR FOR COMIC-CON IN SAN DIEGO, I DRESS UP AS AN EVIL GIRL SUPERVILLAIN. I'D BE HAPPY TO DRESS UP AS A SUPERHERO, BUT THERE AREN'T ENOUGH GIRL SUPERHEROES WITH COOL COSTUMES.

Oh, I just remembered when I was in preschool, a few boys said I couldn't open the pen cap, which was glued to the pen, because I was a girl. So I said I'll show them! And I grabbed the pen. But I couldn't open it! Then the boys tried, and none of them could open it, either. We all laughed.

THE 2010s

- THE US WOMEN'S NATIONAL TEAM DEFEATS JAPAN TO WIN THE FIFA WOMEN'S WORLD CUP, BREAKING THE RECORD FOR THE MOST-WATCHED SOCCER GAME IN US TELEVISION HISTORY.

- ASHLEY GRAHAM, AN ADVOCATE FOR BODY POSITIVITY AND PLUS-SIZE MODEL, APPEARS ON THE COVER OF *SPORTS ILLUSTRATED*'S FAMOUS SWIMSUIT ISSUE.

- THIRTEEN-YEAR-OLD MO'NE DAVIS IS THE FIRST GIRL TO PITCH A SHUTOUT IN LITTLE LEAGUE POSTSEASON HISTORY.

- IN PROTEST OF WHAT SHE SAW AS AN UNACCEPTABLE RESPONSE BY SCHOOL ADMINISTRATION TO HER ALLEGATION OF SEXUAL ASSAULT, STUDENT AND PERFORMANCE ARTIST EMMA SULKOWICZ CARRIES HER MATTRESS ACROSS COLUMBIA UNIVERSITY FOR NINE MONTHS, INSPIRING A NATIONAL CONVERSATION ABOUT SEXUAL ASSAULT ON COLLEGE CAMPUSES.

- THE PENTAGON OPENS ALL COMBAT JOBS IN THE MILITARY TO WOMEN.

- WOMEN'S MARCHES TAKE PLACE ACROSS THE GLOBE IN SUPPORT OF EQUALITY, DIVERSITY, INCLUSION, AND THE PROMOTION OF WOMEN'S RIGHTS AS HUMAN RIGHTS.

- A RECORD-BREAKING 104 WOMEN SERVE IN THE 114TH CONGRESS, THOUGH MAKING UP ONLY ABOUT 20 PERCENT OF THE SENATE AND HOUSE OF REPRESENTATIVES.

- KATHRYN BIGELOW BECOMES THE FIRST WOMAN (AND ONLY WOMAN TO DATE) TO WIN AN ACADEMY AWARD FOR BEST DIRECTOR.

- CONGRESS REAUTHORIZES THE VIOLENCE AGAINST WOMEN ACT TO REDUCE DOMESTIC AND SEXUAL VIOLENCE AND TO EXPLICITLY EXTEND FEDERAL PROTECTION AND ACCESS TO SERVICES TO WOMEN OF ALL RACES, ETHNICITIES, COUNTRIES OF ORIGIN, SEXUAL ORIENTATION, AND TRIBAL AFFILIATION.

- HILLARY RODHAM CLINTON RUNS FOR ELECTION AS THE FIRST WOMAN ON A MAJOR PARTY TICKET TO RECEIVE THE NOMINATION FOR PRESIDENT OF THE UNITED STATES.

- GYMNAST GABBY DOUGLAS WINS THE INDIVIDUAL ALL-AROUND AND TEAM COMPETITIONS AT THE 2012 LONDON OLYMPICS AND BECOMES THE FIRST AFRICAN-AMERICAN INDIVIDUAL ALL-AROUND CHAMPION. SIMONE BILES REPEATS THE FEAT IN THE 2016 RIO DE JANEIRO OLYMPIC GAMES, ULTIMATELY TAKING HOME ONE BRONZE AND FOUR GOLD MEDALS.